Notes from Lea Bailey

Notes from Lea Bailey

ROBERT CHOULERTON

THE CHOIR PRESS

First published in the United Kingdom in 2024 by
The Choir Press

ISBN Paperback 978-1-78963-424-2
ISBN Hardback 978-1-78963-425-9

For James and Elizabeth

Also by Robert Choulerton

Lines from Lea Bailey

Published in 2022 by The Choir Press

ISBN paperback 978-1-78963-271-2
ISBN hardback   978-1-78963-272-9

Contents

Foreword

When writers first see their words in published form, Lesson Number One must be a common experience: It's too late now. Before submitting work, re-read and re-read as critically as you can. This or that piece had been better left out. Just a few, in my first collection, 'Lines from Lea Bailey', I would not wish to preserve.

The more I write, the more I reveal my prevailing style – verses owing not so much to a lyrical poetry as to a prose, sorted and paraded – 'prosems' perhaps.

As one of the 'quiet ones', I enjoy this freedom to wander and express myself over all manner of matters. Even if my observations are at odds with yours, I hope you will enjoy reading along with me.

CONSPIRACY

As if, indeed, so foretold, any centre
Cannot hold, there would seem to be,
If not a guiding hand, then some
Guiding spirit – a spirit restless,
Impatient of a Status Quo: Some sort
Of natural law maybe, something
That verily wishes us elsewhere, and
Other, than this our modern Britain,
Here and now.

Cultural evolution is to be expected
Over time, but the quickening pace,
And the effects thereof, appear to tell
An impatient tale – an unpicking of
The fabric of a Nation.

A certain dismantling seems to be the
Theme, for ironies abound, wherever
These reforming trends are found.

In our Police Service, guarantors of
Law and Order – corruption.
In our Universities, much inhibiting
Of free speech.
In Defence Reviews, shrinking of
Capacity to defend.
From our BBC, obliged to be impartial,
So much subversive innuendo.
Our National Trust, often more inclined

To despise than celebrate our History.
Elements of the Civil Service, less
Inclined to serve.
A fractious Parliament, setting a poor
Example to us all.
And so on.

To be disturbed by all of this, does seem
More than a patriot's paranoia.
Reviewing from here, within – more so
Looking in, from far and wide – one is
Bound to wonder whose interests are
Being best served: Detractors at large,
Potential enemies, those who wish us harm?

Tempting it is, to use the word "Conspiracy",
But this word spawns too many slippery
Images, of shadowy figures, co-ordinating,
Fostering silent treason.
Conspiracies of that kind not very likely,
I hope and feel, but it is uncannily as if
There were. The causes may be doubted,
The effects surely not.

In human affairs it may be so, that a centre
Cannot hold, but new centres must be
Formed, or we revert to anarchy and chaos,
And have to fight for principles and laws,
Over again.
Cultures evolve, I guess, because there is
No better way. Let us build, rather, on
What has gone before.

Let us not scorn the values and ways of
Earlier days, simply to sink them beneath
Our own. Our British Institutions were
A long time in the making.

THE ARMS

To the Hare and Hounds, the Royal Oak,
Methuen Arms and the old White Hart,
What gratitude I owe.
To the King's Arms, the Wheatsheaf,
The Red Lion and the Bell, no less so—
Nor any less the Fox and Badger, the
Nag's Head or the Crown – and others
Of passing acquaintance, in a long and
Meandering life.

How well do such names express and
Recall my personal England; and that
Word 'Arms', for all its heraldic sense,
Has such an implicit embrace and welcome.
I would not like to choose any, above
All, but if I had to, it would be the
Royal Oak, for its very name, it seems
To me, gathers to itself the root and
Spread of English History.

Of English History I am no scholar,
But sipping and supping at the Bosom
Of Old England, in Taverns, Inns and
Locals, I am so much her product and
Progeny – in a sense being nursed—
Nursing my thoughts, half an ear to
Local chat and banter, one-and-a half
To my private musings.

Though the welcome of course is a
Commercial one, it is no less cordial
For that – and the ritual of it all, the
Communal, celebratory ritual of it
All, is no less cordial for that:
You and I depend upon those who
So much depend upon you and me.

But outside, scarcely noticed above
The streets, the Inn-signs bear witness
To fading values and prides – in our
Nationhood, our monarchies, our
Loyalties, faiths, assumptions and
Our rustic ways of life.

Time was, for many generations past,
So much jollier and cosier was the local
Tavern than the average cottage of
The peasantry. Much less nowadays,
With supermarkets fully licensed, and
Centrally-heated homes with Televisions.
So often with gains, are there losses.

But it is devoutly to be hoped, that
Against the trend of 'pub' closures,
There will be a national renaissance,
That generations to come, will re-value
And cherish our mothering Royal Oaks,
Our Wheatsheafs, White Harts, Red Lions,
That they and their children will come
To feel such comfort and gratitude, as I,
For our country's Welcoming Arms.

JASON ALLEN

The turnout at his funeral, from
The Trucking fraternity, showed plainly
What a respected fellow he had been.
Jason, a middle-aged son of
The couple next door, met
A swift and violent death
On the highway. Though a
Latecomer here, I came to know
Him fairly well, for he lived
At home with his parents.
I say 'fairly well', because he
Was a man of few words, a
Man of modesty and reticence.
I think I know a good man
When I see one, and such was he:
All road deaths are tragedies,
But how easily I fall to saying
That Jason's was particularly sad.

Too often do we hear and read
In the headlines, of men
Mistaking coarseness, and
Swagger, for manliness.
But in Jason of Lea Bailey,
Masculinity was worthy of its name.
A strongly-built fellow, he
Seemed to have great inner
Strength as well, calm and
Self-contained, at peace, with

Never a hint of arrogance—
And always a readiness to
Help out people in need.
His was a masculinity good
And simple, without a trace
Of strutting, posturing 'machismo'.

And it is for those simple
Virtues that Jason remains
In the memory, exemplifying
That brand of manhood
Throughout the world which
Properly serves mankind, which
Protects and secures us all,
By dependability, and good nature.

In my mind I have an
Indelible image of Jason, in
His Stetson hat, at the wheel
Of a strongly-built American truck,
One of several vintage vehicles
He owned. Whatever else of his
They have disposed of, Paula
And Douglas, his parents, have
Kept this truck in their yard,
In Memoriam — memento
Of a fine son of Lea Bailey—
And by extension, I like to think,
A tribute to 'Jasons' this world over.

———

Three years now, since Jason and his
Fellow enthusiast, Andrew, died on
Their way to a vintage vehicle Rally,
And nothing by way of redress or
Retribution, no hint of justice to atone
For the sufferings of Paula, Douglas
And their other sons.
Clearly, Jason and his friend were
Blameless, for the ambulance heading
Southwards from Hereford had careered
Across the road into their path, too
Swiftly for them to avoid, striking them
Pretty well head-on.
One of the reasons ambulances, like
Police cars, have a crew of two, is that
You will look out for me, and I will
Look out for you; each will ensure
That the other stays awake.
Yet it seems that both, in that ambulance,
At the end of an overnight shift, were
Drifting off in a doze before that
Appalling impact, which they both
Survived, but killed the blameless two.
Yet now, three years on, it seems that
According to our law, both survivors in
That ambulance were blameless too.

In the absence of any proof to the contrary,
And following all police investigations,
The Prosecution Service of the Crown
Can find no case to put before a Court:
Something other than culpable negligence
Must have led to that collision.

The complications of our laws in cases
Such as these, are well beyond me, but
As a next-door neighbour looking on,
How sad it is to see the distress of a
Mother and father having to accept that
The loss of a beloved son was unavoidable,
Pure accident, just one of those things.

FAITH

I really am prepared to believe,
That you do believe what
You say you believe, however
Supernatural or baseless
It all seems to me. But,
Unfathomable creatures that we are,
I must allow that your belief
May be little more than Hope,
Attaching to a Faith — and
Belief would seem to need more
Foundations and buttressing than this.

Yet, Earthbound metaphors soon
Dissolve, in the solvent of the mind,
Rational thoughts such limited value
To our human kind, millions of us
Swearing by, and finding sanctuary,
In their old, ancestral Faith.

And so, though I cannot
Bring myself to believe, — and if I
Have to 'bring myself' to believe,
Belief must be no more
Than some contrivance—
Nor pretend that I believe,
While clinging to established Faith,
I have to be prepared to see
That what you say you believe
Is indeed what you do believe.

Nevertheless, in all my doubt,
Even when I'm ill-at-ease,
Envying you your certainties,
I can but marvel that you need
Nothing, simply nothing, but
Unquestioning Faith.

CELEBRITY

Even when I don't know, exactly,
Where, or for what, they became famous,
Most of those presented in the media as
'Celebrities', make me wish they
Would go back there, and stay.

The fact that she was an everlasting
Harridan in a TV 'Soap' – or he, a
Talentless stooge, unaware of himself,
Known for uttering silly catch-phrases
Especially written for him –
Conspicuously devalues, and squeezes
All meaning from, that word 'Celebrity'.

Those who crown them thus, and fawn
Around them, have much to answer for:
For garlanded by this spurious fame,
They find themselves as Household Names,
Magnified in the 'Tabloids',
Endowed as 'Personalities',
With a status in our Media World
So few of them deserve, or justify.

It follows that we would love to know
Their family histories, personal tragedies,
Treasure their advice on the social issues
Of the day; we would love to know their
Taste in music; love to see them on
Game shows, or dancing on the Telly.

And who wants to learn of History,
Or Archaeology, directly from the
Academics, when we can enjoy it
Vicariously, fronted by a Celebrity?

Who wants to be shown the wonders
Of the world by a seasoned explorer,
When we can follow some smiling
'Celeb' with an over-fed ego?

ACOUSTICS

Nor, in a silent restaurant,
Can I talk to my companion
In any but the most confidential tones,
Inhibited by acoustics:
Overhearing what other diners are
Saying, I am simply unable
To make so public, the thoughts I
Express to my beloved friend.

And I wonder if the beloved friends
Of those who broadcast their thoughts,
For all of us to hear, are
At ease, or silently embarrassed.

But in my case, the inhibition
Is much the same when meeting
With a mate, over a pint,
In a peaceful country pub—
Inhibited by acoustics.

Not only my innermost thoughts, then,
Not only affectionate tête à tête,
But any personal disclosure
Must be guarded, muffled—
Inborn self-consciousness—
Never to be overheard.

Not sure how much I envy
Broadcasters their free voices,
In restaurant or country pub,
Or how much they irritate me:

I suppose the one gives rise to the other.

KNOWN

From time to time,
In our deepest sleepings,
It is as though furtive
Agents of the mind – benign,
One likes to think – inhabiting
Our vacant spaces, attend
To matters strange, disconnected,
Touching us or troubling us.

Whether by careless chance, or
By purpose, from time to time,
Something of their business
Intrudes upon our slumbers
In plausible cameos, cartoons—
And when it does, we have
No option, it would seem,
Except awaken, find out more.

But agents of a sleeping mind,
By daylight, leave no spoor—
A fading echo, nothing more—
As if so personal is the matter,
Better even we, left to ponder—
So little comfort here, that
We ourselves had best not know
What is known, unknown to us.

KINDNESS

If you have no conscious thought
For your own advantage, in being
Kind, there may be a place for you
On Mount Olympus.
For it would seem that kindness
Towards others is so steeped
In satisfaction for one's self:
Whether the kindness is home-grown,
Secular or spiritual at source—
Never, without some personal profit.

Kindness, then, may seem twice blest,
Though diminished, to be sure,
When the motive is impure—
But how can a motive be impure
When nothing could more natural be
Than the biological betterment of 'me'?
So is conscience rationalised, and eased;
That we have conceived kindness
Is to our everlasting credit, and
What matter, so long as we are kind?

And while we are rationalising,
Invoking all biology, where is
The kindness in replicating?
In its rawness there is none,
In seasonal mating there is none,
In its functional displaying,
In its compulsive coupling,
In its inescapable procedures—
Of kindness, there is none;
Yet there is mutuality.

Independent of the seasons now,
Of fruitfulness and shortages now,
Along come we, appropriating,
Adapting for ourselves
Aspects of the whole procedure—
With Ritual and Romance
Endowing it, adorning it—
With amorous dalliances,
Wherein our very kindness
Stands to lose its innocence.

There is available though, in our love,
A truth, in which offering and
Accepting are the same, kindness
Never self-interest by another name;
Available, a precious mutuality,
In which they are the very same;
In which there is no conscious,
Self-serving thought, but unutterable
Love, the head submissive to the heart,
Dovetailing with its counterpart.

GENIUS

To your attendant genius, he must defer—
Faithful genius; she who guides
(To all but others of that ilk, unseen),
Incomparably wise: To her must he defer.

Having drawn some water from her well,
Walked with her and talked with her,
Listened to and learned from her,
Warmed by the very summer of her,
Borrowed of her thoughts and feelings,
Mine own attendant, made of meaner stuff,
Rebuked now, as he rightly is,
Scarce can look her in the eye,
But genuflects, as is her due.

He will recommend, I'm sure,
That never blocked nor hidden
Must misgivings stay,
But spoken, brought to light—
As in some gloomy room, a sunlight beam
Picks out particles afloat, which
Had passed unnoticed in the air.

So let my sunlight, spoken frankness be—
To open windows, clear the air,
That words may follow where feelings lead,
And not be doubted at her door,
But admitted, allowed to pass
Unrefracted in her glass.

Then might he stand his height,
And be with her in this light :
And then, dear love, face to face,
May they steal a soft embrace—
For are they not, when all is said and done,
Unavoidably two, so compellingly one?

TRIBUNES

Considering duties and functions
Of our Members of Parliament,
There is such semantic shuffling
Between 'Representative' and 'Delegate'
As to suggest those two words
Are contradictory opposites—
So suspicious, these quibblings
Of elected representatives,
Or delegates, in Parliament.

Yet not so opposite, those two words;
Synonyms, as close as clones,
Identical twins – tribune,
Agent, mouthpiece—
They both and each imply
A binding moral duty
To express the wishes and
Feelings of their constituents,
So far as can be known.

Unconscionable then, are
Deviations from this duty;
Unconscionable then, any
Honourable Member—
Knowing the prevailing view
Among his constituents—
Voting to the contrary:
What an insult to Democracy
That would be.

It would appear that, when
A Member first takes his seat,
By some Parliamentary wizardry
He is endowed with insight
And wisdom beyond the
Reach of mere mortals—
When it is plain for the world to see,
Your brand new local MP
Is no better informed than you or I.

Climbing those rickety steps
Of arrogance, is fodder
For political cartoons—
But more serious, much
More important than that,
As well as its cowardice—
Its betrayal of the voters
At the ballot box—
Is its naked immorality.

General indignation may be assumed,
And examples are not hard to find:
From my own personal perch, I see ...
That foreign immigration is welcomed,
Early release of prisoners, enlightened,
Realpolitik trade is honourable,
Defence expenditure, money wasted,
Proportional Representation disastrous,
Capital punishment beyond the pale;
Plebiscites undermine Democracy,
Private education to be frowned upon ...
I wonder for whom they claim to speak;
Seldom do they seem to speak for me.

INCREDIBLE

To the waxing and waning of
Word-fashions, in 'Epochs', I am
Accustomed – the Greaticene,
Brillianticene, Fantasticene.
The Aceicene the Coolicene—
But now am I up to my neck
In one which, in modern phrasing,
Is 'Something Else' – the Incredicene.

A few years ago, the River Incredible
Burst its banks, overflowing and
Flooding all the fields and valleys
Of discourse, frequently
Rising to the foothills, where
We might expect to find phrases
And sentences unsaturated:
'Incredible' – adjective ubiquitous,
Its adverbial form no less so.

Yes, yes, I know, language is a
Living thing, an organism which
Adapts and evolves, but I do wish
Words would shift by creative,
Incremental usage, rather than
Misuse in ignorance, and
Parroted by dictionaries which shy
From being too correct and prescriptive.

The word has so far dragged
Its anchor, as rarely to be
Used in its basic sense of
Being beyond belief: My thesaurus
Offers thirty 'synonyms', from
'Phenomenal' to 'super-human'—
Its adjectival value blunted, stunted,
Every iteration along the way.

Come, let us respect these words
We've invented, for our own understanding;
A vast lexicon is at our service,
So rich in nuance and aptness.
No need for words so blunted and stale:
Let us embrace the habit and pleasure
Of reading – explore and profit from
The bountiful fields of Literature.

PROCESS

Reading back, through our recorded
History, and thinking back, through
Biological, geological history, and
Beyond, how tempting it is, to
See and imagine ourselves
As the ultimate, intended
Purpose and Reward of
Some vast Cosmic Plan—
Pinnacle of Creation,
Nature's magnum opus.

Thus a potent disincentive now,
To focus human eyes just now,
Lest what we have, here and now,
Is the mere cresting of
One evolutionary wave—
Whence another several
Hundred million years
Render our descendants
As different from Homo Sapiens
As limpets or lug-worms.

It seems quite unthinkable
But there you are, I have
Thought it, and written it:
Nor need it be a discomforting
Thought; indeed it may be
A kind of reassurance,
A balm and leavening
Of exclusively human pride—
The most pathetic fallacy of all,
Coming before its fall.

A prospect so remote from us
Within the compass of our minds,
May serve to reassure us all—
Evolution may not be so blind,
Apparently cold, impartial,
Lacking capacity to think—
Yet age by age selecting out,
With relentless, natural logic,
Filtering out, winnowing out,
All our petty vanities.

The which relentless process,
Ultimately benign, refining
All posterity, by and by
Eliminating all corruption,
All impurity of mind—
That our simplified descendants
Are paragons of goodness—
Limpets saintly and serene,
Lug-worms irreproachable,
Grateful, eternally, for their heritage.

SIGNATURE

If you should ask for my autograph,
I readily will oblige, out of respect
For you, that you should pay me
This compliment, returning the
Gesture of friendship, and Lo,
It shall be a passable likeness
Unto my name.

But ask for my signature, and I
Shall be a little less obliging,
A little more wary, for
Signatures –somewhat synonymous—
Nevertheless entail something
Official, accepting responsibility.

This document can be authenticated
Only, exclusively, by me—
And I guess it is this swelling
Truth, that soon possesses me,
Twisting and shrinking my signature
Way past legibility—
Scrambling my actual name
In a scribble of conceit,
Consumed by my own importance,
Flourishing so wantonly
To the point of a careless,
Practised, ostentatious doodle—
To show you just how elevated,
Important and influential,
I am.

MOON

With what poise, and grace, does she
Ride, out there, our supervising moon;
With what understated care, does she
Attend, out there – a lightship in the
Offing.

In apparition only, does she wane—
Assuredly to wax again, while life
Below goes ambling by; life below,
Born to die, insubstantial as the sky.
Rock-constant is our moon, ruggedly
Standing by, as though she hears our
Upturned thoughts.

Howsoever fathered, mothered is our world:
In every mortal memory, a mother lingers,
On recall. It is as if our mother-moon so
Lingers, available to all.

Personify her how we may, exalt or
Even worship her, pronouns imply
A universal truth – mother care enshrined,
Ennobled in the human mind: Our
Ever-constant moon, come what may,
Never turns her face away.

ARTISTRY

She is only a painting, after all,
Hung on their dining area wall,
Yet her appeal to me could
Scarcely be more, were she
Present, in warm, touchable skin,
So faithfully is she rendered,
So touchingly is she rendered:
Though I write from memory,
The image true enough, no less.

She is a dark-haired lady—
Mediterranean, perhaps—
And naked down to her waist;
Seated on a fireside rug,
Left hand to the floor, supporting,
Legs drawn up to her right,
Skin burnished in her fire's light—
And all I'm allowed to see,
Is her back, that's turned towards me.

The rest is left to my imagination:
Sadness at her mouth, perhaps, mystery
In her eyes and general disposition;
Breasts too, formed only
In my thoughts; maybe she
Senses a wistful gaze
Behind her, drawn
By the artist's pigmentation
And spiced, by her very coyness.

My hidden thoughts he seems to see;
The painting I'm left to complete
Can only be mine, and me.
The artist knows, and by his
Artistry, understanding in his art,
Draws me, expresses me, close
Behind that dark-haired lady:
And she is only a painting, after all,
Hung on their dining area wall.

SUSTENANCE

Carnival, Festival, the very words
Are the proving of it:
Is there any commemoration,
Observance, celebration,
Party or ceremony
That does not centre upon,
Focus upon and ritualise
Itself, upon food or drink?
Rhetorical of course, this question;
Worth posing, nonetheless.

It surely has its roots in
Ages so much more precarious,
Desperate, hand-to-mouth ages,
In bare survival times, when
Any successful garnering, plentiful
Fruit or lucky hunting,
Called for a general welcoming,
A vague and humble thankfulness
For every sign and portent
Of some providential power.

When we are Wining and Dining, with
A clinking of glasses and
A gourmet spread, a kind
Of thanksgiving it may well be,
But sounding suspiciously
Like the very opposite
Of comfort and joy,
Masking our abiding Hope
That we are indeed in the care,
Of some providential power.

How salutary, to ponder from
What merciless inheritance
Are we such supplicants now,
And how, with such rituals
By and large we cope
And appease the world around us,
With offerings of food or drink—
And to what extent our rituals
Represent our pleadings,
And manifestations of Hope.

WINNOWING

Laughing being, as I suppose,
Something only humans do,
One wonders why it might be so—
And being so, what on Earth
Gave rise to it: Oh to have
Been witness, way back to our
Awakening, hominid pre-history,
To our dawning awareness
Of foolishness, embarrassments,
So long before such could be given names.

If laughing is nothing but a
Release of some kind of
Pressure, a venting of some
Pent-up nervous tension—
It is everything in our modern
World; incalculable its value—
Adapted well beforehand
Through histories of stress,
A saving faculty for our kind,
Acknowledging all our frailties.

Much faked and counterfeited, we know,
Its authentic, bona fide form,
As of Mother Nature's therapy,
Is visited upon us;
The faculty is not quite ours:
We are less its subject than its object;
Not actively do we laugh,
We are passively laughed—
A winnowing of our worries,
Helplessly shaken of our stresses.

SNOWDROP

Call it Galanthus Nivalis,
If you must, but can there
Be any name for a wild
And familiar flower,
Any name more elegantly apt,
Than 'snowdrop' for a snowdrop?

Notwithstanding its classification
In botanical terms, its nature
Is enfolded in its simple
Country name, a modest, nodding
Harbinger, whispering a hint
That Winter, for now, is fading.

Snowdrop, the name, manifestly
The only name, at once
Seasonal, coy, and right
For such a common flower,
Quietly pleasing, so
Faithfully inhabiting its name.

LEADERSHIP

We who were meeker, un-protesting,
Were the ones, invariably,
Who were told off the most.
Those in charge would give
To their own frustrations, safer,
Freer vent and volume—
Measuring their power
Against our meekness.

Those less yielding, with
Insubordination in their eyes,
A certain insolence in their faces,
Attracted less attention
From those in charge—
The ill-disciplined
Disciplined less, somewhat
In charge of those in charge.

It soon became clear, to the
Tough no less than the meek,
That venting of spleens is never
Enough; leadership calls for
Impartial confidence and courage,
And that naked precepts, furthermore,
Shorn of context and example—
Lived, embodied by those in charge—
Are simply insufficient:
Paramount, that power of personal example.

FINGERTIPS

So many years have ambled by
That now, in my old mind's eye,
The image I have archived of your face,
Should give way to some truer face—
But I will not entertain it:
Those forever features, smiles,
Those youthful eyes of yours,
Are forever mine. Excuse me if I
Hope, dear friend; allow me to
Hope and feel that mine own
Within you, do similarly linger
And there, be no less welcome.

I like to imagine, dear friend,
That memories can touch,
That memories are coupled
As with recollecting fingertips,
Reaching out to touch;
That all moments when I think of you,
Are moments when you think of me,
Fingertip to fingertip—
And that what we both once felt
In our eagerness of youth,
Were no mere frivolous fancies,
But embodied some abiding truth.

MATERNITY

Some years ago, at work, I
Came across a well-to-do lady
Who had just packed her young
Daughters off to Boarding School.
To justify this her conscience,
I guess, spoke, explaining that
If she'd kept them at home —-
And I swear to the truth of this —-
She feared she would
"Smother them with love".
She came into my mind recently
As I listened to Radio Four,
Where a Modern Young Mother was
Complaining, with never a trace
Of irony, nor self-awareness;
Complaining she was, of this
Government's miserly provisions
For child-care: How did they
Think her husband's salary would
Support them and their toddler
If she did not go out to work
To afford the child-care fees?

Expecting now a second child,
And facing double the fees,
This Modern Young Mother, who
Seemed to think that money
From 'Government' grew on trees,
That tax-payers across the land

Should support her babies
While she pursued her career,
Seemed to think that nurturing,
Developing, loving and preparing
Her babies for life was
A public responsibility, not hers.

In the muffled new mind of
This Modern Young Mother,
Her mission in life left children
As a nuisance, inconvenience —-
A barrier to success.
However impoverished their young souls,
No matter; Modern Young Mother
Would enjoy a fulfilling career.

Well, what of the Modern Young
Father, I hear you asking?
A Modern Young Question, I know,
The very posing of which
Highlights attitudes shifting
With each generation,
Each new cohort apparently more
Enlightened than the one before.
Looking back on a long life—
I am writing in my 'eighties'—
I've seen nothing to suggest
That the paternal instinct is,
To the maternal, even comparable.

We can all quote exceptions,
Which, by definition, do but
Confirm the general case—
Such as this Modern Young Mother,
And the lady who packed her
Daughters off to Boarding School—
It is not a matter of
Scholarly logic or reasoning;
It is a matter of common
Observation, and sense.

It seems an odd perversity,
To ignore biological truth,
And the insistence of evolution
In female anatomy for the
Bearing and suckling of young—
An unsurprising consequence of
Which, is inherent mothering instincts.

If both father and mother are there
At home, it little matters,
But one at least, must be there, in
Those precious, crucial early years,
And for Pity's Sake, let it be she.

LAUNCHING

When you have launched your book
For printing, it is out there, on
Its own —- too late now to
Correct the punctuation, choice of
Words, the phrasing, emphases,
Fitness for purpose in the
Critical readership out there,
All of which were within your
Power to make good, if only ...
If only you had spent more time
With your child, loving the child
Into confidence, resilience; endowing
Your child with social eloquence,
The socialising grammar and
Seaworthiness, out on these oceans
Of citizenship, fellowship
And critical readership:
After launching, it is simply too late.

INCOGNITO

I recall, from my childhood, sentries
And patrols by night, wary of infiltrators,
Would challenge, "Who goes there?
Advance and be recognised!".

A harsh comparison, I know, but
Brought to mind by the occasional
Man silhouetted, as it were, against
The brighter, affable majority:
Such a man I encountered briefly,
In a store in Gloucester.

He began each sentence with
"To be quite honest.", talking at me,
Chiefly with his voice, smiling
Chiefly with his mouth, and when
He strutted off, I noticed that
He walked chiefly with his legs
And feet: The human being was
There, sure enough, but the
Personality had some fear of
Advancing and being recognised.

EPITAPH

In one of his broadcast 'Letters',
That matchless commentator on
American affairs, Alistair Cooke,
Related some history of prospecting
In the rugged, frontier, pioneering days.
Particularly moving, he found,
Was a wooden notice, above
The grave of a young pioneer
Who had succumbed to the
Toil, and the icy wilderness:
With stark simplicity, the
Notice read, "He Done His Best".

I too, was moved, well beyond
Many more effusive epitaphs
I have read.

In an office where I once worked,
A fellow came one day to
Service some faulty equipment—
A northerner he was,
With an easy, affable manner.

At one point, reflecting on daily
Work and duties, he said,
"Y'do y'best, daunt ye"—
As if it hardly needed saying;
As if 'owt else were unthinkable—
Who could question such a
Benignly simple philosophy?

The beauty of those words
Remains with me,
Lingering about my conscience.

What fleeting glimpse was this,
Of pure and obvious guiding principle
That hardly needs articulating?

If not sedimentary trace,
What moving power this, of
Uncorrupted, prelapsarian Grace?

HEDGEHOG

Call it Erinaceus Europaeus,
If you must, but can there
Be any name for one of
Our native mammals – any
Name more befitting and apt
Than 'hedgehog' for a hedgehog?

True to its classification
In Latin terms, this pussy-footing
Forager-by-night, itself a
Diminutive hedge, with sensitive
Snout and piggly gruntles,
Backpacks its own insurance.

Creature of covert and thicket,
It verily names itself;
In simple truth and modesty,
Seems quite content in private life,
Snuffling about in the darkness,
Faithfully living its name.

PHANTOMS

Like every other mortal
Human Being, I am
Operated from a skull, within
Which are housed what
I may call my Headquarters,
Ageless and imponderable—
Where sediments of old
Are tested unrelentingly
By accretions of the new—
Essence of Raw Material wherewith
We have risen, or fallen,
According to your point of view.

Being so constrained, and
Imbued by these Materials Raw,
Creatures in and of themselves,
Knowing little of themselves, and
Even less their seminal spawning
Consequent to Earthly dawning,
I can hardly blame Headquarters
For my dumb perplexity:

Manifest truths, such as
Gravity, Night and Day,
Consequences having Causes,
I can reasonably grasp.

But remaining stubbornly
Beyond my grasp, and with
Little guidance from the skull,
Numerous Phantoms haunt,
Defying the senses, never
To be apprehended, as if
To tease and taunt ...

Such as the Edge of Space,
Everlasting Life, Open Prisons,
Ritual Circumcision, Infinity,
Spoiling Ballot Papers,
The Big Bang Theory,
Cheating in Games and Sport,
The "Meaning" of Life,
And Transubstantiation ...

These by no means all,
But some, for the moment, I recall.

FLYORITY

Yet again, at the Annual
General Meeting of the Congress
Of Migrating Wildfowl,
The matter of plane-strikes
Headed the Agenda: Was
There nothing could be done
To rid our skies of shrieking,
Featherless aeroplanes?
Yet again, the Sponsoring Goose
Set out the well-established case:
"Delegates must be weary of
My repeating it, but it is
A matter of Simple Precedence—
From aeons of evolutionary
Aviation law; ancient rights of
Flyority are laid down, through all
Migratory flyways in the sky;
Our case remains unanswerable—

How dare those upstarts
Complain of 'bird-strikes';
Dammit, they are 'aeroplane-strikes';
Who is intruding upon whom?
How dare they seek means
To scare us off, or train up
Renegade Raptors to pester us?
How can they complain of
Hazards to their passengers
And their profits, while

Many thousands of our
Migrating Members, day by day
Are slaughtered in our skies?"

The Motion being, as usual,
Solemnly and heartily endorsed,
The President announced the
Much-anticipated outcome of
A total ballot of CMW Members:

"The outcome is unanimous, of course—
No Motion easier to endorse—
Avian advice to human kind:
Have faith in evolution, Nature
Making sense; just wait until
You develop feathers and wings, to
Join the Flyority of our skies,
Learning to navigate by Nature.

What is this infernal haste
Of yours? You miss and
Lose much more than you gain,
By scorching through our skies
Against the will of the Wild.

Peacefully, quietly, sail the seas,
Help to save this planet thereby,
Forget the flyways until you
Can fly; regain your sanity and
Save the precious lives of birds thereby."

SERENDIPITY

Dear Maxwells, Hertzes, Marconies
And all of your kind,
Do not be offended when
I compliment you in two
Contradictory ways – firstly
Of course, for your harnessing
Of electromagnetic waves,
Allowing us to communicate
Instantly with peoples
All around our globe—
But secondly, oh please
Understand, for waiting, and
Not doing so, until late
In our nineteenth century.
For I try to imagine, and
Dread to do so, what if all this
Mass distraction, all too
Often crass distraction, had
Swarmed over us in earlier times?

With round-the-clock TV coverage
Of local skirmishes and scandals,
Michelangelo may never have
Begun, let alone finished,
His Sistine ceiling. With the
Bard himself surfing the
World-wide Web the whole
Day through, we'd never have
Smiled at Bottom the Weaver,

Nor agonised with Hamlet;
With Milton beguiled
By celebrities and game-shows,
We would never have witnessed
Paradise being lost.

With Beethoven besotted
By thrillers and quizzes,
No time for a Pastoral Symphony;
No time for Impromptus nor
A Trout Quintet from Schubert,
Inveterate soap opera follower;
No time for dreamy Nocturnes
From Chopin, absorbed by
Late-night foreign films.

So thanks for your patience,
Physicists all, twice-over blessed—
That those exquisitely-gifted people
Were born, excelled, created and died,
Before your technological tide.

EXPENDITURE

Unavoidable, in our language,
In any language I dare say,
Are illustrative words, loaned
From one context to another,
Figures of speech, tropes to
Illuminate our meanings—
And there you have several already—
One of the commonest of which
Is to speak of 'spending' one's
Time: How did you spend your
Day, your week, your life?
However casually employed,
That word does seem to
Insist on expenditure of life,
Of our time, being a transaction,
And seems also to wonder
If your outlay, your investment
Has been profitable, especially
On the lifetime scale; what
Did you purchase with your life?

We have no alternative but to
'Spend' the life we are given
As a token, redeem it how we will.
Had we somehow 'earned' this life,
This asset, by our own labours,
We might value it more, but
We did not; it was 'given',
Handed down to us at birth.
I wonder whether spending what's

Not earned, but given, imposes
Or removes an obligation,
Wisely to spend our lives:
Several early years we spend,
Before we know and feel that
Our time, our life, will end—
And wonder what will be the
Gaining, the Goods on which we spend—
For profit or loss, for whom
Or how best, should we invest,
In exchange for our precious lives?

Nought for ourselves, of course,
For we shall surely pass away;
Our hopes and regrets, pleasures
And sufferings just ebb away
That very day, with us to our grave.
While for those who ever knew us,
Especially closely, our worth
Will be accounted, weighed,
In their memories which, one day,
Will similarly ebb away.
The clearest way, I'd say,
Investments are realized,
Made tangible, lies in what
We contribute, practically create;
What we leave behind, bequeath—
By paintings, pottery, sculpture,
Handicrafts and carpentry,
Composing works of music,
Novels, plays, poems maybe,
Not forgetting, the occasional baby.

SEATING PLAN

When you host a luncheon party,
Do take care with your seating plan:
Alternate placings, man next to
Woman, then she next to a man;
And if you are able, male
Facing female, across the table:
It will be your only chance
Of open, refreshing conversation.

For when you adjourn from the table,
Five will get you ten,
Women will re-join women,
And men will bind with men.

Then when you take your afternoon stroll,
Five will get you ten,
Women will walk with the women,
Men will make do with the men.

What has Society been thinking of,
One wonders, to insist upon
Synthetic pairings, so revealed
In gatherings such as these—
One man, one woman, in a
Screened-off, isolated life?
Security, privacy, the theory goes.

But human nature will have its way,
And five will get you ten,
Women will always be women;
Men can be nothing but men.

CHAPTER AND VERSE

So long formed and adapted
As we have been, to live
In tribal groups, societies,
Certain necessary traits
Have arisen within us—
Traits and attributes such as
Comradeship, co-operation,
Consideration, loyalty, kindred spirit—
That what pleases your neighbours
Is simply that which pleases you—
A condition which in latter days
We recognise as Common Sense.
It takes various forms, of course,
According to circumstance and culture,
But there resides in human groups
An instinct for what is right
And beneficial for mankind.

All of which makes me puzzle
And ponder, why so many peoples
On Earth cannot think what
Is right and good to do, but
Must look it up in a Book—
Or if they can't read it,
Or still less understand it,
Ask to be told what the Good Book says
About how they might mend their ways.

What is this great faith we have
In our superior selves – that we
Are so elevated, lofty, exemplary—
Yet to know how to conduct our lives
We must look it all up,
Look ourselves up, in a Book?
This very need for a Book
Pronounces our Plight.

Who on Earth would presume
To write such a Book?
And upon what Authority?

Furthermore, to whom
Attribute its enthronement, its
Global, sacred, infallible status?

People, merely people, no more
Entitled than you nor I,
Purporting to be Holy Agents
Of Pure, Almighty Powers,
Somewhere beyond the sky.

And to what desperate needs
Are we to concede this
Universal thirst, for such
Beguiling creeds – ironies in
Human kind, such superior beings
As supplicants—
Followers of Light and Truth,
Or Blind being led by Blind?

THE BOSS

Self-confidence, they say, is
Half the battle, but they
Under-estimate the case:
If you seem to believe in yourself,
With firm conviction in your voice,
And facing people eye-to-eye,
People are apt to believe in you;
People will believe you care,
Assume your inborn abilities—
And a little luck will see you there,
Up at the head of your Company,
Where possibly somebody else should be.
Not that I'd prefer up there
Somebody lacking in self-belief,
But self-belief backed by
Manifest competence, wisdom
And generous personality—
Somebody I'd look up to.

Crucial and fundamental,
In selecting a Leader, is to
Bear in mind that Leadership
Implies a Following; to
Consider the people the Leader
Will be expected to lead.
Mostly, I concede, organisations
Get it right, but it's where
They don't, that's bothering me.

We can all give examples of
People promoted, elevated to
Positions beyond their obvious worth,
Beyond all our understanding,
Right from the minor official
Up to where it seriously matters:
If a President like that,
A Prime Minister like that,
A Commanding Officer like that,
If any like that can come through,
Where ineptness is so costly,
The Selection Process is clearly failing.

The Selection Process is All,
And the earlier begun, the better:
To filter and tune for the
Most promising array of
Competence, integrity, personality—
An aspiration, having Human Nature
In its way, easier posed than answered—
Not least because the Selectors
Themselves may be where possibly
Somebody else should be.
In any effective Process, the
Shallow, the pompous, the honey-tongued,
Will fall at the very first fence.
And the confident voices of those
Who stand out, clearly endorsed
Amongst their peers.

For only when Followers'
Aspirations are expressed, will we ever
See Leadership at its best, and
Stand a chance of avoiding
This aloof Commanding Officer,
This faint-hearted Prime Minister,
This Liability of a President.

LITERALLY

We should be able to use them
In the classroom, verses like this
As teaching aids, these daily
Solecisms – and I mean
Literally daily – on the airwaves
And in the press, such as "Prices
Have literally gone through the roof."
We might ask whether they
Bashed through the roof tiles
Or helpfully used the chimney—
Or might it have been a
Figurative expression, not
Literal at all, meaning that prices
Rose much more than expected?

We should be able to use them,
These daily solecisms – and I
Mean literally daily – on the
Airwaves and in the press, such
As "Literally beating my head
Against a brick wall", hoping
That the ambulance crew were

Able to staunch the bleeding,
And that the NHS was able
To recommend psychiatric help—
Or might it have been a
Figurative expression, not literal,
Meaning you were utterly frustrated,
Finding no sympathetic response?

By all means say that prices
"Have gone through the roof",
Or "Beating my head against
A brick wall"; the words make
Every-day common sense, along
With thousands of similar
Phrases in our language—
Just don't call them 'literal',
Which converts them into nonsense,
And reveals that you don't know
The difference, 'literal' from 'figurative':
Reach for your dictionary
And look up these important words;
Better check out 'solecism' too.

LEAKING

I suppose there must be some
Purpose in leaking to the Media,
Beforehand, all the key points
You intend to make in your
Speech tomorrow —- but I search
For it in vain: It seems less
Likely to encourage attendance
Than make us wonder why bother.
We've heard it on the News,
Read it in our morning papers—
Why would we attend, knowing
What you are going to say?
In any case, leaking rather
Undermines all that personal
Touch in public speaking,
Threatening to starve the world
Of all rhetorical eloquence
In the ancient art of oratory.

Of course I can understand its
Usefulness to the Media—
Hungry, thirsty for Headlines
To announce, and instinctively
Shape the News – while it
Would seem only to encourage
A curious public taste for
All this silliness, very much
Akin to "So-and-So is expected
To be named tomorrow as

England Manager", and of course
Tomorrow, he duly is.
There are enough perplexing
Anomalies in this world,
Without superimposing these.

And although the words are written
For her, I feel a sad discourtesy
To our gracious Queen,
In leaking beforehand, details
Of her State Opening speeches.

And as for yourself, you could
Do us all a great favour:
Keep the speech to yourself
Until you deliver it. We will
Gratefully contain our patience
Without feeling deprived, and
The Media can be left
To salivate, and sit in the
Audience with the rest of us.

UNUTTERABLE

In a modern spirit of benevolence
And inclusivity, a Circular on
Vaccination was issued, not only
In English but in twenty-eight
Other Tongues.

Some, in kindred alphabets
I can roughly pronounce, if
Barely understand; others,
Through Hellenic to Cyrillic
I may guess at — but beyond,
Eastward, lies obscurity,
Where outlandish hieroglyphics
Bar the way – unutterable
Scripts defy my tongue, my
Lips, my voice, my mind; all
My faculties combined fail
To form nor syllable nor sound.
A world of common humanity,
Uncommonly cleft by script
And language.

As meaningless to me, these
Signs and ciphers, so must
My plain English be, to readers
In Samarkand and Chengdu—
Impenetrable Runes – defying
Their tongues, their minds,
To render syllable nor sound,
Outlandish hieroglyphics:
Westward, lies obscurity.

And thus is one abiding truth
Emphasised, made manifest—
That quite as much by utterances
And our scribing of them,
As by Geography or Race—
As so many travellers will attest—
East ever will be East;
West ever will be West.

RIVER

Then go, dear friend, to River's edge;
Sit there quietly on her bank;
Simply watch, and listen,
Allowing your thoughts to flow.
Stay still there, for a year or so,
Witness the passing of Time,
In all the stillness of Time.
Rest there for a hundred years,
Witnessing seasons come and go,
Come again, pass by again—
As people have watched and
Listened there, through ages past:
River will seem to pay no heed,
But hush and ripple by,
Water-coloured by the sky—
Inherent, incidental giver,
Lending life to all about her,
Being, quite simply, River:
She exists, and that is all,
We but likewise, in her thrall.

Riverness, with never a pause,
Incorporates what light there is,
As do we ourselves. The difference
Is, we know of it, and ponder it;
Unburdened River simply flows.
Likely it's a kind of envy
That draws us to sit and
Listen and watch, envy of
The insensate, the self-possessed.

Communing by her side, dear friend,
We pay a kind of homage—
Some air of kinship draws us there,
A belonging, and a longing,
Allowing our thoughts to flow,
As some riparian refrain,
Calling us back home again.

KEY

The 'key' to understanding ourselves
Must be the most obvious word
Figuratively, to focus upon the
Literal, the actual, metallic,
Locking and unlocking key—
Without which we could not
Survive, in modern society.
It does, really, seem as vital
As that, when you pose some
Silly questions: Why, when you
Go out, you lock the doors of
Your house; why overnight, you
Lock your car; why lock away
Your valuables and personal,
Confidential items dear to you.
What? Someone might sneak into
Your house and steal things? Someone
Might drive away your car? Even
Steal your money and precious
Things of sentimental value?

Yes, yes, so sadly, yes.
Even though these things
Do not belong to them?
But isn't that dishonest, and
What's more, against the law?
Yes, yes, so sadly, yes.

It would be of some comfort
To be able to say, in a way,
Such people do not understand
What is right, what is wrong.

Nought for our comfort, sad to say,
For in our pursuit of a civilised
World, we've somehow left
Behind, along the way,
Burglars, thieves, criminals,
Fully aware of right and wrong,
Fully aware of their crimes—
Such a depressing sign of our times.
More than this, we live in times
Of 'organised crime', widescale
Operations, apparently
Devoid of conscience, set up
To deceive and rob us all.
In the light of facts like these,
What can we possibly do
But manufacture keys,
Grim signs of the times, indeed,
Daily condemnations of our kind:
Along with Security Services,
Police Forces and prisons, keys
Are such potent tokens and
Reminders, that our journey is
Barely begun, very far from done.

Keys, locks, locks, keys
Witnessing day by day how
Little we are along the way—
Combination locks, keys and safes,
And it follows from these
Then keys for lockable places
To keep safe our very keys.

Perchance one day, some day, may
We design such a wonderful key—
Unlocks the good in all humanity.

DOORSTEP

I imagine that when, upon
Opening your door, you find
Your Member of Parliament
Standing there, sporting a
Bold rosette, seeking
Your endorsement and your
Vote – I imagine that your
Surprise somewhat robs you
Of your voice. The very
Moment for you to unburden
Yourself of your worries is
The moment you are least
Able to. A certain native reserve
And courtesy may not
Always be a blessing, if
The colour of his rosette
Inhibits you from making
Clear your personal point of view.

Doorstep canvassing is a poor
Substitute for a secret ballot.

Furthermore, the few who do
Pour out their thoughts may
Speak to him of matters too
Contrary, too contentious,
Beyond the pale of orthodoxy,
Hardly worth consideration.

I think on these things when
Your Member of Parliament,
Who'd have us believe he has
Stood on pretty-well every doorstep,
Is interviewed by the Press:
"What I'm hearing on the doorstep",
He will confidently report,
Amounts to motherhood and apple pie.

Far from anything as base and
Vague as border controls,
Security, defence, illegal
Immigration, what he's 'hearing'
Upon hundreds of doorsteps
Amounts to motherhood and apple pie—
The immediate needs of hard-
Working families, to which you
Nor I could ever take exception.

And how often, how predictably it
Chances, that those prevailing
Concerns of his constituents
Reflect, uncannily echo and
Validate measures and policies
He has advocated for so long.

JUBILEE, LANE END

The sounds of forty or fifty folk
From the new marquee, in the
Grounds of Lane End church,
Are mainly the sounds of women-folk—
As no doubt it has so been,
At such gatherings down the ages,
And no doubt ever shall be.
Jubilee moments such as these,
Offer a glimpse of country life,
A country's life behind the scenes
Apparently far from the centre of power.
But this is, here lies, the power:
These are the scenes, personified
Here in the new marquee – living
Proof, as if we did not know,
It's women-folk who run the show—
Fundamental truth, the whole world
Over; their family sense, natural
Domestic womanly network,
Female fabric enfolding us all.

Good-hearted couples, like
Jim and Janet Morgan, will
Organise, supervise and
Lend a hand, but this is
A woman's world in here:
Comparatively speechless, men in
Here, less at ease, out
Of their element, brought along
As added proof or ballast,
Listeners and props, as no
Doubt it has so been, at
Such gatherings down the ages,
And no doubt ever shall be.
For the most obvious goodness
In the human heart, is most
Eloquent in the female part—
And how well do gatherings
Such as these, express common
Purpose, fellowship, community,
Beyond the reach of written words.

Hardly space for the 'waitresses'
To squeeze between the tables,
With extra sandwiches
And pots of tea:
Uninhibited banter, without a
Trace of coarseness, celebrating
Not only Her Majesty's
Platinum Jubilee, but for
People like you and me,
The privilege of living in a
Land as free as a Land can be.

BULLPEEP

For the preservation of culture
And good taste, unacceptable
Or naughty words are known
As 'expletives', routinely
Deleted, replaced by asterisks
Or blocked and substituted
On the BBC News, by
A virtuous, tuneless bleeping tone.

Just as today, to protect the
Ears of British listeners,
BBC Radio gently sanitised
The comments of a US reporter
Who felt that one account of
Recent events on Capitol Hill
Had been total 'Bull(peep)':
So often are blunt realities
Softened by 'peepings' such as
Those, or tip-toed over in
Parentheses such as these.

Curious business, all of this,
For our whole world well
Knows just which word has
Been officially disallowed,
By arbiters of good taste.

Not that I'd rather hear them,
Nor see them in the nude—
But it makes me wonder why
Are particular words so eschewed.
Why, for example, 'dung' will not
Do – ordure, droppings, manure—
Not even 'pony and trap'?
But it has to be a word
That people should not hear.
And why, furthermore, must
This 'peep' be excreted
By a bull? Why not a pig,
Or a goat, or a cow?
Why not cowpat, or cow(peep)?

I guess even 'pig(peep)' lacks
The contemptuous power of 'bull(peep)',
Nor the pellets of rabbits, nor
The ploppings of sheep will
Quite do the trick, when
Compared with the bellowing
Defecations of bulls:
Just a sign of disapproval
After all; well, rather more;
In this account of events
On Capitol Hill, to nobody's
Surprise, there had been little but lies.

But talking of sheep, and words
Which fit, and benefit, I've
Always admired the consummate wit
Of the writer of that nursery-rhyme
Of the shepherdess who lost her sheep:
Rather than offend us with her name,
Spared us the rustic truth of it—
Thought better to call her Little Bo(peep).

CAFE

I never wondered why it was so,
That place I used to head for,
That café above the bookshop
Where I'd go when the shopping
Was done; I never wondered
Why it was so, why it was the
Place to go, why you couldn't
Always find a seat – until I came
Back to the town, after a couple
Of years away.
With such fond memories I
Hurried there, when my shopping
Was done, and then, that shock—
When it dawned – just why it had
Once been so, the only place in
Town to go: For the place I recalled
Was no more; the place had been
De-humanised. It was a café area
Still, for sure, but they've tidied it
Up, that café where so many used
To meet, above the bookshop, above
That busy street.

They've cleaned it up, tidied it up,
Rearranged the tables, more orderly
Now, more sensible now and overseen,
Put new lighting in, made a brighter,
Open plan of it, made a less than
Woman and man of it.
Vanished, that old ambience, that
Informal atmosphere where you could
Feel at ease, chat in confidence, not
Feeling observed or overheard – a
Cosy, agreeable place, briefly your
Very own space.
Evaporated, the soul of that place,
Along with its welcoming service
At the counter and the feeling that
You sat where you chose: Something
Of a different sort, less for people
Than for customers and clients—
Quieter now, emptier now.

If your café is 'buzzing', year after
Year, something must be right,
Whatever it is. Leave it be. It's not
'Buzzing' to be more orderly and
More brightly lit.

This was once the place to go, and
It was the shoppers, up for their rest
And their coffee who made it so—
Not prescribed for them but expressed,
Characterised, humanised, by them.

In the tidy minds of some, there seems
To reside a law, to disapprove of what
Has gone before.
Often do our rational minds mislead us;
As often do things turn out best, when
Instincts, natural feelings, are expressed.

GLOSSARY

Lines in verses, in poems,
I like to think, arise not to
Illuminate themselves, but to
Bring into particular focus
Thoughts and feelings for
Their readers – but lines and verses
That will not yield their meanings
Without glossary and explanatory notes
Merely masquerade as poetry.

If they deploy foreign phrases
Rarely seen in common use;
If they delight in references
Pretentiously arcane, we
Might infer their purposes
Less to enlighten and inform
Our simpler souls, than to
Draw attention to a writer's education
And intellectual pedigree.

Glossaries, explanatory notes
Completely give the game away:
'Poems' that cannot speak for
Themselves are impostors, not poems.

And the ingrained irony
Of it all, shines forth: Why
Bother with the 'poem' at all
If the understanding or the benefit
Lies in the glossary, the explanation?
We might as well study these,
And regard the verses, the
'Poem' as supplementary notes.

COMMITTEE

Once more, the Chairman has
Declared the Meeting closed;
The next, one month from now,
Come what may. Once more, as
We leave the table, minor meetings
Break out among those hitherto
Silent, listening to the eloquent few.
For once more, the eloquent few,
The usual confident few, had
Carried the Meeting through, while
We silent ones wrote the occasional note.

This is the way of Meetings, the
Way they seemingly have to be:
If all eighteen of us spoke,
Speaking correctly through the Chair
In third-person terms, endorsing or
Challenging the confident few,
Meetings would be three times longer,
Or rather the Chair would intervene,
Leaving much unfinished business.

Or else there is, in human gatherings,
Some innate and necessary faculty
Providing for, allowing for, expediency
In human affairs, the only
Workable, 'default setting' – some
Residue, maybe, of the biggest and
Strongest passing on their genes.

Judgement and wisdom, everybody
Knows, are hardly confined
To life's eloquent few, yet how often
Their insistent voices carry the day:
What is heard and thought, but yet
Seldom said, would seem
To sort the leaders from the led.

Nor are these disparities
Entirely evened out when
The Chair calls for a show of
Hands; a show of hands
Isn't quite a secret ballot.

The next limitation will come
With the distribution of the Minutes,
When we learn what we broadly
Agreed upon in Committee, by and
Large reflecting less the force of
Argument, than of personality.

And so we await, for another
Month or so, when the Chair will
Declare the next Meeting open, to
Gather around for an hour or two,
And listen to the eloquent few.

CONVENIENCE

Cousins came to visit, one day,
When I was a young boy :
That's when I first heard it
Called a 'toilet'. In our house
It was the lavatory, the 'Lav', where
We went to 'do our business'.
Luckily, ours was indoors, with
A cistern up high and a chain to pull.
Many places had 'closets' or
'Privies' out in the yard; a
Few still had no flushing at all,
And routinely had to improvise,
As did the whole world over,
Every single day down the ages,
Since we all began.
Out and about, I learned that
'Gents' was where I had to go.
It stood for 'Gentlemen' – an
Optimistic word from some time
Past, distinguishing the noble
From the great unwashed, implying
Honour, courtesy, refinement.
Be we never so common, coarse or
Foul-mouthed, we used the 'Gents'.
The 'Ladies', similarly, echoed an
Earlier social status – Lords and
Ladies – elegance, refinement,
Even in the act of emptying
The bladder or the bowels.

There was nowhere else for us
To go – no places set aside
For the Hoi-Polloi; we were
Ladies and Gentlemen.

Gradually, but insistently,
Came social shifting and
Re-appraisal: Gentlemen, Ladies
Outmoded, too prescriptive and
Formal for the purpose, and the
Vernacular, in any case had long-
Since made its own way, spreading
The public discourse, from delicate
Euphemism to wanton coarseness—
Facility, Powder-Room, Water Closet,
The Loo, Khazi, Dunny, The Bog,
And onwards into gratuitous smut.

So the 'Gents', 'Ladies' morphed
Into classless 'Men' and 'Women'.
And then the feminist lobby took
Exception to the logos at the
Entrance for the women, replacing
The prim, skirted, legs-together
Image of womanhood by a more
Spread-legged, androgynous look.
The label 'Toilet' lingers on, both
For sit-downers and stand-uppers,
Somewhat upstaged these days
By 'Facilities' and 'Conveniences'.

At the time of writing, it is just
As much the labelling of the users,
The public, the clients, that bothers
Trendy people. In these gender-
Neutral days, even using 'Male' or
'Female' for some is too old-fashioned
And divisive. Yes, toilets at home
Are gender-neutral, but at home there
Are no total strangers in the Lav.

So far have we travelled, that this
Daily animality of excreting our waste
Has embarrassed us into privacy;
So numerous are we now that
Sanitation and sewerage are
Essential to public health.
And so self-important have we become
That public places for natural, daily
Voiding of urine and faeces, and all
We who must use these places are
Flattered by discreet and powdered wording,
As if to disown ourselves.

This is no Lav; can't you see it's a
Civilised, respectable Convenience.
So does our social history unfold, and
'Wash your hands afterwards', we are told.

THOUGHTS

I wonder if there were ever any
Original thoughts, before mankind
Started making tools, dabbled in
Language, made patterns on cave walls:
Before those awakening moments,
All was instinctive, I imagine—
Though the moon, the stars,
Rainbow and thunderclap, the
Seasons, relentless light-time
And dark-time, must have lent
Some dread and stirring of curiosity
In creatures with a rare potential
To perceive and apprehend.
And now that we have 'minds',
And some say even 'souls',
Worldwide steeped in languages
And clogged with learning—
Libraries, archives, non-stop
Broadcasting, a smothering
Of communications to fill
Anybody's lifetime,

I pity the baby, the child,
Born, endowed with but five
Senses, blind instinct for mimicry,
Raised with such diminishing space
For developing thoughts of its very own.

No need to ponder, then,
Why we, in all creation,
We people must take holidays:
No other creature on Earth
Seems to need to take such a
Break, relax, refresh, allowing
Some space for personal musings
Even rudimentary thoughts—
Strolling by some desolate shore,
Pausing at the forest edge—
New life crawling, leaves a-falling,
Sweet and saddening intimations,
As if of some ancestral calling.

PUCCINI

There is no need to understand Italian,
To appreciate an opera by Puccini, for
The words are in his music for us all.
By all means browse, beforehand,
Synopses of his operas but never, please,
Seek help from subtitles in English; all
They can do is stand in your way.
Subtitles in our English tongue—
Operas indeed, English language sung—
So freighted, Earthbound in our native
Idiom, do scarcely leave the larval stage
As opera, or so it seems to me, for
English is my only tongue.

On the other hand, it seems to me,
The very soul of Italy lives in the
Lyrical candour of its language—
Animated conversations in every
Home, on every street, libretti in
Themselves, anticipating opera.

Puccini hears their music, and
Lifts them to his purpose, words
With music wed – Dragonflies and
Butterflies in Drama, articulating so
Much more than simply may be said.

For all I know, the idiom of their
Houses, on their streets, stands
Between Italian and Puccini,
But I verily doubt it so,
For well beyond the reach of words,
Music serves us all, meriting all the
Homage words must perforce to music pay,
And what more natural homage,
What greater compliment from Puccini,
Than echoing what his people say.

ROUTINE

Seldom, I guess, has a holiday
Been so refreshing that it was
Not a relief to get back home,
Back to domestic Routine—
For Routine is where we belong.
It is our very birthright, for
From Routines are we derived—
Daytimes, night-times, seasons
Of our sun and moon, themselves
From vaster ones derived:
How could we be else
Than creatures of Routine?
And how, furthermore, could we
Fare, without our man-made
Yearly timetables? Each year
Itself foretold by our sun, but
The naming, numbering of months,
Weeks, days, are contrivances
Of our own, for the sanity
And ordering of human lives.

With no timetable, without diary,
Clock and calendar, there is no
Town or city, no commerce, industry,
No organisation, no schools,
For Routines are of necessity born.
No paradox this, in human affairs,
But plain common sense, that
Within Routine lies our Freedom.

Only within established limits
Can we be Free: Routine is
Custom and Ritual by a more
Familiar name, it seems to me.
Routine – inherited prescription
As it were, for people's well-being.

And so a Holiday makes no sense
Without that from which it is
A refreshing break: The one
Defines the other. Beyond Routine
Lies not Freedom but Chaos,
As every fervent anarchist
Will find, creeping back home to
Domestic Routine, with the rest of our kind.

PM DEBATE 2022

In the announcing, anticipating
Of the event, you could already feel it:
The two aspiring Prime Ministers
Will not meet face-to face, but will
'Go Head-to-Head', invoking stags
At rutting-time, or frenzied
Capercaillies at the Lek.
To expect the rivals for the
Highest Office in our land to
Exchange views in civilised,
Respectful terms, it seemed,
Would be simply too naïve.

Almost, one could hear organisers
Licking their lips; more audibly so
The journalists: Ahead of the event,
One unashamedly wrote "Sunak must
Drop the courtesy and rip Liz Truss apart".

Head-to-Head then, it must be,
In the fair, democratic way, on
Television for the world to watch.
But further, in the journalistic way
Also, must be theatrical, staged,
Compered and dramatized,
Before a selected audience.

Along with several million others
I listened and saw, through my
Old prejudices filtered it all and
Weighed it in my mind:
Self-conscious of course the rivals
Were, under such spotlight and focus,
But they gave a good account of
Themselves, revealed their differences
For us all – a fairly animated encounter,
But with far too much talking over
Each other, and discourteous interrupting.

It was only on the morrow,
On the Radio, in the Papers,
That I learned what I had missed:
'Barbed' and 'acrimonious' at the
Least, it had been; the 'vicious'
Candidates had 'swapped blows';
They had been 'at each other's throats',
'Knocking lumps off each other';
They had been 'at daggers drawn'.

One wonders what standards and
Principles they imbibed as students
In their Schools of Journalism, and
Whether the curricula had ever
Included objective reporting.

CRITERION

'Institutionally Racist', this Company,
Concluded the Report, commissioned
After several complaints, as a
Result of which, the entire Board
Resigned. The Report objected, it seems,
To the Board being institutionally White
And, to the modern urge for Diversity,
Being institutionally blind.
If the complaints and the Report
Were right, we might expect Selectors
To set examples and choose Directors
By criteria free from any racial taint—
By experience and wisdom only.

A tasty touch of irony then,
That the Report should recommend
Constitution of the Board by quotas:
Fixed proportions of black, and brown
And white people – the overriding
Criterion? Selection by skin colour – Race.

WOMEN'S EURO, 2022

In this Final, rather like the men's,
There was plenty of talent on display;
Plenty of skill on the ball, passing
And attacking flair, rather like the men;
Multiple petty fouling, rather like
The men; remonstrating with the
Referee, rather like the men; a certain
Petulance too, reminiscent of the men—
The women's game, differing from
The men's, mainly in its name.

Clearly the better team on the day,
The 'Lionesses' deserved their victory:
Why then could I not dance a merry
Jig with the nation's celebrations?
Could it have been that I'd wished
The Lionesses to lose? No, not quite
So. That their standard of play
Would be embarrassingly low? No,
Not quite so.

That I'd wished their game more
Distinguishable from the men's?
Closer, maybe, though not quite sure,
But something stood between me
And outright rejoicing.

For I seem to stand as prisoner in the
Dock, self-accused in the curmudgeonly
Court of masculine vanity – a barely
Conscious dreading of some kind of
Redundancy, a sense of peripheral
Uselessness, in a world where muscle
And aggression no longer hold sway—
Where more and more are we
Diminished, taken down, standing by,
Occasional, for mating, something
Along these lines, maybe.
Who are we if we cannot affect some
Specialness, posture and display,
Pretend to some significance and
Splendour beyond ourselves?

What are we if womenfolk can
'Out-posture' us, upstage and
'Out-man' us – show us that we
Are nothing special? Something
Along these lines, it must be.

Nothing special indeed are we,
Just naturally male and vain.
Should this trend continue,
And our vanity prove too stubborn,
Where next we may turn to
Flatter ourselves – which turning
Next where women may not follow,
Or what sharpening of behaviours,
Should give us pause.

LOOKS

They matter so much, do Looks—
To follow the fashion, conform
And bend, to the cultural trend,
Wherewith we cover, present ourselves—
For the stark, embarrassing truth
Is that cover ourselves we must,
For with few exceptions we are
Bound to admit that uncovered,
Exposed, in our birthday-suits,
We amount to not very much:
Better announce ourselves by clothing,
Topped and crowned by a
Carefully carefree head of hair,
Not merely grown but 'worn',
Rather like stylish headgear.

Outward shows, clothing and hair
We may say, essentially being the
Signs and ways we give ourselves away.
Both, at once, concealment, cover,
And speaking on our behalf.

And let us admit, in adorning
Ourselves we are not entirely free:
Only up to a point may we dress,
So insistently does our culture press.
Each culture has its 'uniform',
And the token of its membership
Is to be appropriately dressed.

How clever of people then,
Of such necessity to render virtue,
Exploiting our disguise
To tell our personal tale before
An array of people-watchers' eyes,
With a dab or two, a badge, a buttonhole
Here, a ribbon, a clasp, a pendant there,
And more and evermore these days,
Tattoos to draw the admiring gaze,
All in the name of Vanity Fair.

REVERIE

A writer is no better than
Anybody else, just so much
More distracted, that his
Fantasies will keep pestering
Him until he sets them down,
Somehow has to set them down—
Like coming across that lady,
In the Department Store, that
Lady he knew years before,
When she served behind the counter
In his local village shop.
His recollection was true enough;
His fantasy thereof the stuff
Of fiction, wishful thinking, and
A certain pathos of the lost:
And so it is that now
I happen again to meet, in my
Mind's Department Store,
That lady who works in the
Village shop no more, for that
Post Office shop has closed down now.

And of course she is widowed now,
And seems very pleased to
Come across this fellow again.
It follows, in my mind, that
My suggestion, that we should
Have a coffee together, would
Be very welcome; she could do with
A sit-down after so much shopping.
It follows also, in my mind's
Coffee shop, that she would
Love us to meet for lunch,
In a nice restaurant or pub:
The scene merges into that
Deeply satisfying lunch, and
Hopes, mutual hopes, that
There are sweet and tender
Moments beckoning us,
Totally absorbing us, until
I am roused, so unkindly roused
From my writer's reverie, to
Do my washing-up and to
My shopping-list for tomorrow.

ANONYMITY

A lovely photograph it is, of
My daughter-in-law and the
Two children, on a short visit
To Tarragona; although for the
Purpose briefly posed, seizing
A quietly happy moment—
But I couldn't help noticing, to
My left of the photograph, a
Rotund local fellow was about
To cross the lane behind them—
Incidentally, involuntarily
Caught, trapped, recorded;
However blameless, guiltless
He may have been, arrested
In mid-stride.

Just one of countless millions of
By-standers, completely unaware,
Snared since photographic lenses
First cast their nets with meshes
Too fine to respect everybody's privacy.

It is one thing when the camera
Surveys from afar, with multiple
'Extras' at some distance,
Quite another when the 'extras'
Are close by, as if intended
Subjects of the photograph,
Immediately known and named
By all family and friends, but
Quite unknown and unnoticed
By the camera.

Of no consequence at all, this
May be, but if it were you, and
If it were me, we might like to
Know who has captured our image,
However innocently, who has
Caught us unawares, recorded,
Archived for posterity, in whose
Private files we rest in peace,
Nameless, incognito, immortalised.

LETTERS PAGE

Some editors, it's fair to say, will
Openly use the active voice, but
Others still will stay behind the
Passive, in warning of their rights
To what comes close to censorship:
By nameless figures behind the scenes,
Letters may be edited.

To having my letters edited, I am
No stranger, mostly by provincial
Press, but in national papers too.
Treatment has ranged from weeding
Out adjectives, which I accept, to crude
Evisceration, which I do not—
Even to modify a point of view—
Editors far from coy or being impartial:
Editorial, their power.

Prepared as I am, to accept their right
In legal terms, to tamper with my letters,
Their right in moral terms is what I rather doubt—
It is too precious by half, to insist
That 'letters must be exclusive'—
Fancy, readers of some lesser journal
Able to read what is in ours—
Revealingly weak and insecure.

What right to change the wording of
A letter, for their readership far and wide
Then attribute this amended letter, still, to me?
There must be a case for some extra attribution,
Identifying this wielder of presumptive power.

And it would be worth knowing, on
Any Letters Page, which ones – especially
From people in 'high places' – are verbatim,
And which are not. This could easily be
Earmarked so: Writers would appreciate
Such a courtesy, and readers could treat
Letters with a little extra caution.

VULPES VULPES

If we can find it in our hearts
To forgive a spider its spinning
Of sticky webs to entangle
Its unfortunate prey;

If we can find it in our hearts
To forgive the limbless snake
All its covert, deadly stealth
In seizing unsuspecting prey;

If we can find it in our hearts
To forgive the tawny-owl its
Lethal seeing-in-the-dark, silently
Snatching its hapless prey;

Then why there are those among us
Unable to forgive our native
Fox its predatory instincts,
I am at a loss to say.

Why there are those among us
Determined to pursue and kill
Foxes with packs of hounds,
Encouraging and harnessing in
Those hounds the very instincts
For which the unforgiveable fox
Must die, I am at a loss to say—
And from what I've heard of
Their justifications, so are they.

And yet, and yet, I'm bound to say,
Aspects of their Meets, their Hunts,
Completely give their game away—
Splendid in their hunting livery,
Proud upon their hunting horses,
Entitlement, they radiate; appearances,
Rituals must be observed—
As clearly well beyond the killing
Of foxes, with slavering hounds,
Other statements must be made,
Wider purposes must be served.

COMPARISONS

Suppression, they concluded; what
Else could it have been but
Arrogant suppression of females
Down the years – that most, by far,
Of the world's greatest composers,
Painters, playwrights, poets and
Sculptors were male – the assumption
Being that if only men were not
Such overbearing pigs, females
Too would have created works
Of equal genius. This proposition
May seem sound, but stumbles
In that cul-de-sac, Comparison.

Down that dark alley of Comparison
It is never easy to see; it has such
High walls, admitting so little light.
So seldom can it compare, fairly,
Like with like, so often can it confuse
Cost with usefulness and value, and
So often see rivalry where there need be none.
Few things more futile then, than
Compare, indignantly, womenfolk
With men. Female and male:
Attributes so spread as to overlap,
Yet inhering still, ways essentially
Female, essentially male.

Then to allow that the greatest
Literature, the finest symphonies
And works of Art—
Far from expressing exclusive
Talent in the masculine sex,
Likely spring from weakness
More than strength; likely
A sense of redundancy and
Worthlessness, undermining
Nature's strut and posture:
The further from the Wild into
The civilising world we progress,
The more must we dazzle to impress.
One recalls how often we find
That so many eminent artists,
Composers, poets, had been such
Unlikeable oddities, self-regarding
'Misfits' in their day – closer than
 Coincidence, I venture to say.

The female, I hope you can agree,
So much more self-possessed:
From such needs relatively I say,
Relatively free is she: Of creating,
In the artificial way, much less need—
Or so, from this distance, it seems to me.
For fundamentally, what can be
More fulfilling than childbearing,
Or the potential thereto – and the
Giving of birth; what can be more
Creative than this – never to be
Known by any male.

Never, never, can a novel, a play,
Concerto or a Sistine ceiling serve
A higher purpose on this Earth,
Than nourishing an infant from its birth.

Plenty of scope for good humour
And banter, in Comparisons and
Differences, but it is to a wonderful
Common purpose that we are so
Divided: May mutual respect and
Understanding be our guides.

HARDCORE

In the pastures of erotica, the
Term 'Hardcore' is as ill-suited
As it is misleading.
On second thoughts, maybe
It is unintentionally apt.

Twice in my lifetime have I
Cast eyes upon such – the
Second merely confirming the first:
It thrives by naked masquerade.
It promises. Knowing its promises
Are empty, it promises still, for
There is, in humankind, an
Ever-ready market – the abiding
Lure of a promised land, hidden
Treasures, exhilaration, consummation,
Forbidden fruit. And that word
'Core' suggests an essence, a root,
A revelation, being, in this context,
Nothing of the kind.

What Hardcore reveals, above all
Is its own mendacity, as if the
Natural act of coupling, in humankind,
Were insufficient in itself, but must,
By art and artifice, be enhanced,
Refined, packaged, made saleable, sold.

And so, through the pastures of
Erotica, the term 'Hardcore' becomes
Its own irony, leading us nowhere
But to Bathos – way beyond, way
Short of, gentle arousal and fondness,
Utterly detached from love,
To a bleak, anatomical absurdity.

FLAG

Most of the time, it's the Union Flag
They fly, next-door; sometimes, when
England is in need, the Cross of
Saint George they fly, and on occasions
They hoist to the breeze our Naval
Ensigns, White for the Royal, Red for
The Merchant, reminding observant
Passers-by of seafarers, past and present,
The guardians of our seas.

Just so, worldwide, do flags articulate
The broadest, even vaguest, of
Allegiances and sentiments of nations,
Which are not reducible to words,
Accruing to themselves a wealth
Of symbolism, representation—
Vicariously, they proclaim for us.

Few things more exemplify and
Bitterly illustrate this than enemies
Of a state ostentatiously burning
Its national Flag —

And how potent – lowering to
Half-mast the Flag of a nation
In mourning, hanging its
Head in sorrow.

They speak in headlines, do flags;
They speak in principles, expressing
A nation's purpose, and values.
Such is their symbolic power
That we salute them – ritually,
We salute our flag – a loyal gesture
To a symbol, a country, a cause.
Yet the permanent display, next-door,
Of our national flags, open expressions
Of national pride, is so noticeable,
By being so rare.

Even today, an England, a Britain,
A United Kingdom, by nature
Inclined to reticence, would
Rather hide its feelings.

Three cheers then, for my next-door
Neighbours, for maintaining such a
Churchillian stance by flying our
Colours, reinforcing all we know
To be true: Some things are worth
Fighting and dying for.

The freedoms of our people are
What we fly our flags for. Freedom
Is what we stand for; Of this, the
Whole world can be sure—
Our Union Flag its guarantor.

QUEEN ELIZABETH II

Involuntarily, tears welling,
Oddly enough not at the
Long-expected news of Her
Majesty's demise;
It was the tide of sorrows
And praises, simple or eloquent—
Spontaneous heartfelt eulogies—
That so brought tears to the eyes.

And so, to people far and wide,
Such a conduit and courier
Of goodness and grace was she,
Devotion to Duty personified;
Ever ready to reconcile, with
Receptive, reassuring eyes
And that ever ready, warm
Authentic smile.

No malign, mean or selfish
Thought, could ever have found
A lodging in this Lady's mind,
Which had rooms only for the
Joy and betterment of mankind:

It seems to need a rare and
Open Medium of her kind
To call forth kindred goodness,
Impulses kindred in us all
Which so often lie suppressed
Perhaps for fear of seeming
Weak, or soft.

That it should take the death
Of our Queen to unclothe our
Common feelings, remarkable enough—
But more so the exposing, the
Accepting of our common Destiny
That melts us all down: Nor charm
Nor virtue grants exemption; our
Tears are for ourselves, as for the Crown.

ANTICIPATION

Having never met before, yet were
We no strangers, it was clear.
How our eyes did smile, quite as if,
Met before, they truly had.
As if wordlessly they knew and spoke
Before did we, before our clasping
Of hands. There was a homecoming
About it, a grown-up adolescent tingle,
A breathless recognition, a finding of
That long-lost glove, a winning prize.

To spell out your virtues would be
To recite my very own leanings and
Fancies, as subjective and personal
As ever can true love be.
Blind and wondrous Chance then,
We must believe, our two paths
Should cross – so late in the Day,
Our stories all but told. What is
This evening now, but ours to share?

This evening now, is ours: Eventide
Shall not rule; she shall but wait upon
Us, at our leisure. Let me light our
Candles, yours and mine, and to
Some gentle nocturnes ...

shall I dine, and gaze into that
Vacant space, contemplate your
Absent face, those conjured eyes,
That smile evoked and summoned
Up in such a wistful trance,
Fickle, fantasy partner in this romantic
Dance – imagination, fortune, Chance.

But thank you, all the same; at least
I have your company in the while.

Whatever it may be that renders
Us susceptible to dreams, dreams
Are less our purpose, I suspect,
Than our fate; less the dreamers
We be, than pliant instruments
Of those dreams. How they play
Upon our fancies and ambitions,
Teasing hopes and expectations,
Seducing us from reason.
How often is the journey sweeter
Than arriving, the appetite tastier
Than the food. Is not each human
Life, indeed, one great anticipation?

So once more I thank you. Vigilant
And patient I remain, until by Chance
Our lonely paths might cross again.

TABLE FOR TWO

The essential business of this world
Is conducted, transacted and agreed,
Not by some Supreme Conclave on
High, General Assemblies, Super-Power
Summits and their Communiques – but
In a million quiet, private meetings,
Between the likes of me and you,
Across a table reserved for two.

Exclusive restaurant, corner café, downtown
Diner; in the country pub, the private Club,
The rendezvous is the Table-for-Two: It's
Not the à-la-carte menu, the sandwich, the
Coffee, the ale – it's the Table-for-Two, the
Private, confiding tete-à-tete, just between
Me and you. It's the occasion, the moment,
The conclave of two, a leaning-forward
One-to-one, where much of the work of
The world is done.

It's behind the scenes, at Tables-for-
Two, where many a deal is sealed,
Many a friendship forged, many a
Policy honed, a plan refined, contacts
Briefed, secrets leaked, a rumour
Confirmed or denied – sins confessed,
Promises sworn, confidences shared,
And many a lasting love declared.

Each Table-for Two encounter, as one
Tiny cell, we may say, innumerable
In our times, one tiny cell of which
The tissue, the body of human affairs
Consists, serving to bring the greatest
Affairs of State down here, where
You and I may play our part, have our
Say, understand and contemplate.

CENTRE GROUND

There is no map nor compass in this
Political wilderness, to tell where may
Be found, that ever-elusive area,
Centre Ground. Even if stripped of
Every nuance, reduced to flat polarity
As 'Right' or 'Left', so elastic are these
Terms: Centre Ground can only be
Implied.
'Left', after all, is left behind, abandoned,
While 'Right', as not being wrong, is
Fraught – to which we must add a
Tendency to attribute meaner morals
To the Other Side: Centre Ground can
But be implied
And here lies the handiest means, for
A journalist to pose his moderation,
In the face of dark extremes.
Imagine just for a moment, if you
Can, that a BBC newsroom were
Left-inclined, then it may help you
Understand why the term 'Right wing'
Is not quite pejorative enough—

'Hard Right' is better, 'Far Right'
Scarier still, and the more often
Repeated, the further to the Left
Is the Sensible Centre implied and
Nudged: What is 'Far' but way out,
Extreme and dangerous.

Then to this poisonous label attach
Such poisonous trends as being
Anti-immigration, clearly signs of
Nasty xenophobia: Odd how rarely
Are 'centrists' and Left-wingers
Dubbed pro-immigration, and odd
How rarely we hear the term 'Far Left'.

Then to this same sticky label attach
The term 'Populist', a word which
In recent years has had all notions
Of virtue beaten out of it—
(Popularity, popular, meeting with
General approval... in a Democracy?
Whatever next?)—
Meaning now something like an
Approval only by mindless 'Nasties'.

Mindless indeed, must we be, if
Through all this egregious nonsense
We cannot spot the disingenuous,
Shifty journalism squatting on and
Marking with its scent a bogus
Centre Ground, shaming its profession.
Being as directional and opposite as
East and West, 'Right' and 'Left'—
As evaluators – may not be our best,
Too temptingly employed as tokens
Of morality – 'Far Right' as hateful
Brutality implying, in the mind, 'Far
Left' as virtue and gentleness.

More illuminating, less susceptible to
Party dogma, would be to revive the
Old political colour-coding – redness
For socialism; capitalism as blue – some
Mixed economy as Centre Ground.
These colours being Differences, not
Opposites, here are nuances affording
Centre Grounds less for the journalists,
And rather more for me and you.

FOLK

For all the distractions of our
Modern age, deep and distant
Echoes tug at us from time to
Time, recall, evoke our pre-
Industrial, even pre-historic
Selves, when it seems we were
Essentially 'Folk'.

Fables, Tales we told ourselves,
Ancient superstitions grew and
Grow upon us, identify us still
Essentially as 'Folk': Folk dances,
Folk songs, Folk tales endlessly
Survive while fashions come and go.

Original pathfinders in the wild
They must have been, a taking of
Bearings, locating ourselves in the
Wilderness, making sense of our
Primitive selves.

More substantial than nostalgia,
'Folk' is of our culture. To tug at
Us is to touch us, recognise us
Through the ages: Who cannot
Be touched by the loving faith
Invested in a Corn Dolly, that
It may secure the next year's
Harvest? Loving faiths this world
Over, today as yesterday, so much
Part of who we are. Dancing and
Singing, nowadays as thenadays,
We keep our spirits up against
An indifferent world.
The word 'Folk' links us to living
Off the land, to the rustic, to crops—
A grim peasantry over-romanticised
I guess, in modern times, envied
And celebrated nonetheless.
Our word 'Folk' would seem to me
Somewhere, in a way, we'd rather be—
As though we've strayed too far from Home.

TEDDY

Even having only one cub at a time,
Such maverick mammals are we that
We do not sleep with it snuggled in
Beside us; even if we suckle it at our
Breast, from the outset we consign it
To a separate nest. For much of its
Crucial early life – so that we can get
A good night's sleep – it has to suck
A dummy teat, snuggle a dummy
Mother, out in its separate nest.

Especially now, with the unexpected
Legacy of a cartoon depicting President
'Teddy' Roosevelt as a cuddly baby bear.
Especially now, is the baby deceived,
Cuddling Teddy, a surrogate, a hybrid
Quite unlike its mother, but baby-like,
With a bear-like face, not down on
All-fours but shaped to sit and stand
Like you and me, in such an appealing
Manner – no paws nor claws, but with
Hands and feet padded for a baby's comfort.

If it must have a separate bed, kinder
Might it not be, that a cuddling surrogate
Resemble the mother instead – lest in
The attic of nursery memories, the
Favourite toys, the old cub's cot, old
Teddy the more remembered, the
Mother the sooner forgot.

Slim hopes now, I suppose, with a
Teddy-bear, a baby bear, generations
So imprinted.
Unlikelier still, we rediscover our
Mammal selves, incubation running
Its natural course, cub delivered,
Suckled and weaned there, in the
Maternal nest, the due separating
Therefrom when both mother and
Cub, instinctively, know best.

MEME CREEP

It must be the truths they embody,
That make our proverbs stand the
Test of time, such as this one in
Pursuit of proof, so well worth
Repeating: 'The proof of the pudding
Is in the eating', traceable back to
The fourteenth century.
Too often, even so, is the oral tradition
Mislaid, as if failing that test of time,
Losing its point, its truth, along the
Way. Nowadays I hear nothing about
The eating – the 'proof' mysteriously,
'Is in the pudding'. Some irony, that
Integrity of tradition by word of mouth
Be loosened in an age of literacy.

About twenty years ago, I first heard
The saying, 'If you want something
Done, ask someone who's busy',
Surprising and well-observed advice.

Only a few months ago, I heard it
Curtailed in Woman's Hour: 'If you
Want something done' said the
Presenter, 'ask a woman who's busy',
Which retained the paradox, while
Implying the idleness of men.
More recently still, I was sad to hear
The subtle point of it missed completely:
The lady said, 'If you want something
Done, ask a woman'.

We may smile indulgently to hear
These sayings hollowed out—
Amendments far less likely to stand
The test of time – far from conscious
Modern refinements, let us say;
Misunderstandings, more like.

We may rest assured that proverbs
Will hold fast, standing the test of
Time, available for the quoting, their
Truths forever proved and reinstated.

BUTTERCUP

Someone, in the English-speaking
World, first joined them, but
These words, 'cup' and 'butter'
Suggested themselves, naturally
Enough, for this common meadow
Flower.
'Butter' and 'cup', homeliness and
Sustenance evoked in a meadow
Flower – a cup-like blossom with
The very complexion of butter;
Butter indeed from the very meadows
Where they thrive: Just as well
Cattle grazing their meadows
Find them bitter to the taste.

'Butter' and 'cup'; how well they
Sound and suit together, an
Unlikely pair, coupled in their
Context, felicitous as can be:
Ranunculus Acris, alias Buttercup.

APPELLATION

No need to hear the voice; the first
Name will usually do, female or
Male, a pretty infallible clue, so
Allocated are first names – by
Familiar usage of course – but a
Listing of girls' names and boys'
Names shows them often variants
Of each other: Nigel and Nigella,
Norman and Norma, Daniel Daniella.
Revealing also how commonly,
Male names end with consonants,
Female usually with vowels, often
With extra syllables: He is Patrick,
She Patricia; he Henry, she Henrietta.

How this came about, I can merely
Speculate, wondering what attributes
Of the sexes gave rise to these word-
Clues, sound-clues. Well preceding
Fashion and received usage must
Have been some utterances befitting
Female, befitting male.

Hearing, the other day, people
Railing against modern parenting,
Brought all this to mind. They
Deplored any biasing socialising
Such as toy trains for boys, pretty
Dolls for girls; football for boys,
Netball for girls; trousers for boys,
Dresses for girls – let them discover
Themselves, was the plea.
That the lady leading the crusade
Had a son, Callum, a daughter
Alicia, names as socialising as can
Be, names as likely to signpost their
Futures as any nursery toys, did
Seem to undermine her cause.
On reflection, maybe kinder than
Naming her daughter Bert, and
Her son Fiona.

KISS

As one of the sweeter adaptations of
Our human kind, it belongs to us, does
The kiss, ever since we stood our
Height; ever since our female turned
To face, enabling this, our humanoid
Embrace – and as our verbal language
Grew, a language of expression too,
And this sweet language of our lips.

To kiss does seem an exclusively
Human thing to do, yet feels as
Rudimentary as can be, primitive
As a baby presenting to its mouth
Whatever is at hand – our mouth,
Our lips, such ageless samplers.

A certain impertinence, I fear, in
Theorising a kiss, but it lives with
Us from beginning to end, marking
The family, the lover, the friend.

We may not understand, but there
Is no true loving, in the human sense,
Without the reassurance of our lips.
To kiss is to caress: In the loving kiss,
Mutuality is of the essence, mutuality,
Tenderness. In the loving kisses are
Requests and reassurances, offers
And yieldings; lip-speak, lip-language
For aspiring lovers, beyond the reach
Of spoken words.

And so a certain reverence is due,
Consistent with the moments and
Their meanings.
No more should we expect to bellow
Our lust into a lady's ear, than subject
The hapless lady to any oafish mouthing
Manifested in the name of 'snog':

Listen, and feel how much more
Respectful, genuine and fitting, in
Our human context is this gentle
Meeting of lips so aptly rendered
In our language, as a 'kiss'.

BIRTHDAY

It's not as if we were volunteers:
Mute essences were we, coiled in
That pulsing darkness there, potentially
Formed and shaped until that day,
From darkness into light expelled, with
No choice, but an incoherent voice—
Labelled with a name, to begin to age.

As our Birthday, unsurprisingly, is
That day known. And though we
Could hardly help being born, as
The years are counted up – or
Counted down – each anniversary
Draws congratulations, as if for
A personal achievement.
This datum-point, our Date of Birth,
Demanded of us nearly as often as
Our names, is of constant interest
Wherever we turn – what age are we—
Everywhere a human awareness of
Beginnings and endings, with a
Pathos seldom recognised.

For it's not as if we are volunteers:
Ageing is our lot, subject to waxing
And waning, circling the calendar
And our sun, with happy returns,
Surviving by instinct and hope,
Clutching at Culture, each Birthday
Celebrated, a fine achievement.

Unconscious echoes, may much of
This be, of child mortalities in ages
Past – that with special cakes, presents,
Parties and blowing out of candles
We celebrate Birthdays, and that
The occasion is a happy one, not
Only for the achiever, but for all
Well-wishers too – with the singing
Of 'Happy Birthday to You' one of
The brighter and more poignant
Stitches in our human tapestry.

BLESSINGS

With what due reverence do we
Wander forest aisles, slaking of
The silence, open to the peace,
The guidance, the blessings, as
If, of something close to sacred
There, we are aware – some sense
Of kinship, abiding sermon in
A forest air.
A bird-call here and there, and
The hushing of the breeze,
Point the silence and the power
Of those trees. Within the stillness,
Beneath their vaults and canopies,
We ourselves fall silent,
As if in silent prayer.
However poor in spirit we may be,
In a forest there is healing,
Whereto such reverence is due;
In the bosom of a forest are
Beatitudes, blessings and balm
For every questing human mind—
Blessings of the natural kind.

STANDARD-LAMP

In the corner of the living-room
The standard-lamp grows proud,
Human-high; nor can the very
Hardwood base itself bear to be
Featureless and plain, but must
Characterise and brand with
Circular reliefs and scoops,
Centring on, securing, such a
Robust bobbin-shape as footing.
For proudly does the upright grow,
As any plant to seek the light,
With scarcely any part that does
Not claim its natural right.

At every stage a circlet bound, as
If each does from the stem beneath
By nature spring; calf-height, as
Thigh-height, fluted for a texture,
Reaching, flaring and tightening,
As of human limbs – no more a
Perpendicular pole, shorn of its
Woodland soul—an organic
Form once more, knee conceived
As an ancient urn, with such floral
Grace; at the head a slender goblet
Form, around which the craftsman
Chose patterns of leaves to trace,
And budding lips.

The 'trouble' he took was clearly
No such thing, but devotion and
Care – more a rite, an observance,
Than a piece of work – natural
Shapes, familiar forms – all to mount
Electric light, several feet above the floor,
Making one wonder quite what
Design and art are for.

Further to his wonderful skills of
Hand and eye, some void to fill
Perhaps, remembrances may be
And, I sometimes think, some
Sub-conscious cri-de-coeur.

PMQ's

And so between a nature and a
Culture are we poised; which
Be the substance, which the veneer,
Beyond any doubt.
And so we look to people in the
Public eye and public service
To take a lead, exemplify, in
Both their private and their
Public lives, all civilities, manners,
Courtesies – making others feel
At ease, exalting by these means,
Our enlightened species.

And so where better than in
Parliamentary discourse, to
Deploy such noble qualities: There,
In the Mother of Parliaments, before
The public gaze – for the exercise
Of politeness, and generosity of
Thought between Honourable
Members, no more opportune stage.

And so it follows that weekly
Prime Minister's Questions times
Are Heaven-sent for opportunities
To show respect for opponents,
Putting them at their ease ——-
And opportunities abounding to
Make such a clamour that we
Cannot hear what a Member is
Saying — to ignore twice or thrice
The Speaker calling for order—
To recall with glee every past
Misjudgement an opponent has
Made – to take every chance to
Embarrass a Member, howl with
Derision at every slip of the
Tongue – to interpret an opponent's
Words in the meanest possible
Way – to deploy sarcasm, and
Revel in signs of weakness or
Discomfort – to concede nothing,
But cynically doubt and snub an
Opponent's every point of view.

And so it is, they park their
Veneer of Culture at the Commons
Chamber door, that listeners and
Watchers can know them in the
Raw, more clearly than they did
Before.
Do they just play at boorishness
For entertainment? Is it all a
Harmless venting of spleens—
Or democracy by some other means?

It is worse than all of these:
A veneer has been peeled back,
Sure enough, but what it reveals
Are not blameless instincts—
For the essence of this depressing
Spectacle, the entire show, owes
Much less to natural history than
To humanity in disgrace, calculated
Spite, shaming our Parliament,
Our people, our race.

CONTRADICTION

It lasted about a second and a half,
His gesture, such a brief moment,
Yet quite enough to lodge in the
Memory. As a member of the
Tennis Club Committee, he strolled
Into the office, where there was a
Document for him to authorise:
Inseparable from him strolled his
Sense of professional status, among
Lesser folk.
Without a greeting, he sat down
Before the document to be signed,
And paused, drawing attention to
The fact that we had not provided
A pen. This did he wordlessly,
Without looking up, but formed his
Fingers as if holding a phantom pen
Above the paper; a brief twitch of
His fingers mimicked a signing.
Whatever it was that stood between
Him and a simple request for a pen
Was something to ponder.
Such a contradiction it seemed—
So full of himself; unaware of himself.
Wearing his self-importance as a
Regal vestment, but blind to its
Transparency. A General Practitioner
By trade he was, generally confined,
Bound inside, blindfolded by ego.

Self-confidence is a wonderful thing,
When stopping short of arrogance;
Self-awareness admirable too, until
It keeps us from the best that we can
Do, the kindest we can be.

How to find some optimum path,
Between these two, some middle way?
Perhaps to see ourselves reflected
In a story, a film, an opera, a play—
Or reading some writing, such as
This, here, now, today.

PARTICLES

Were we nothing more than chemistry,
Wrought from basic particles,
Whereof this wide world teems,
We'd be nothing more than elements
In some human Periodic Table—
Sorted into groups and periods,
Valencies, properties, potentials,
Limitations.

Were we nothing more than chemistry,
Why, we'd find that some people
React freely with others, while some
People are rather isolated, rather shy,
Aloof.

We'd find that some take to water
More readily than others, that some
Are rather sharp by nature, others
Emollient, inert and mild; that some
Incline to the left, some to the right,
Others transiting in between.

We'd see elements gather themselves
In families, or tribal groupings,
Merging their identity thereby.

We'd find that some of us are more
Stable than others – some with longer,
Some with shorter lives – while others
Shift from one condition to another—
Just supposing chemistry was all we were.

GRACE

Or take the case of those two
Children — about ten or eleven,
As I recall – secretly saving together
From meagre pocket-monies, to
Buy for their uncle a Christmas
Present, a Compact Disc.

And take that moment when they
Handed it to him, gift-wrapped,
Wishing him a Happy Christmas.

And take his response, on opening it:
His oafish manners simply amplified
His voice, defiling that purest of moments—
"OOHH! OI O'READY GOT THAT ONE!"—
Nought for those children in his
Joylessness, not a sign of exemplary
Grace for their young minds.

Then take his response to their offer
Of selecting another CD—
"WOULDGERMOIND?"

Whether they did so or not, or
Minded or not, I cannot report,
Memory numbed and frozen,
I suppose, by that man's crass,
Abominable bad manners.

To this day, I wonder how it can
Possibly be, that anyone could reach
Physical maturity, in such a state of
Blind insensitivity.
But it will do no harm to remind
Ourselves that from time to time,
Amazingly, so, so sadly, it can be.

RAINBOW

Nobody else in the world can see
That Rainbow that you can see; that
Rainbow belongs to you, as mine
Belongs to me. Each Raindrop in
The sun identifies us, one from one.

The focus and location of yourself,
So personal is your colouring, from
Your violet to your red, from your
Hopes to your loves, your tastes and
Temptations; from your fears to your
Tears, wherein reflected be your soul—
Exclusive is your Rainbow.

Of your own unique, internal reflection,
Your Rainbow – your particular arc
In this world – with much beyond the
Visible – that is your light in every
Stormy sky, and the light for us to
Know you by.

GODFORSAKEN

Deep in their godforsaken forests and
Wildernesses, those benighted aboriginal
Peoples thrived, unknown, untouched by
The restlessness of civilisation, untouched
By insatiable Wanting and Searching.

Indulgently, we came to know them as
Lost tribes, which knew no better than
To thrive on no more than those forests
Could provide – along with countless
Other forms of life – the forest organism.

Nothing did they know of weeks or
Months, simply times of light and times
Of dark – a life in thrall to the Forest
Mother's call, her echoes, her spirits and
Her multifarious scents; Mother supplying
The foragers' every instinct, every need
As to dwelling, breeding, and dying;
A satisfaction in her bosom, and a canopy
Beyond which no human mind need stray.

While others, and others, went forth and
Multiplied, and multiplied, and civilised,
Until rapacious needs never could be
Satisfied without setting their loggers,
Their miners and their bulldozers upon
Those godforsaken forests.

And what of those godforsaken people,
No longer lost, but liberated, exposed
To the lights of learning and reason—
Rootless, homeless wretches, so sadly
Unaware of their own abysmal ignorance,
Who never drew wages, never had a
Holiday, never knew their rights, never
Had ambitions or careers, never played
Ping-pong, or polo.
Those godforsaken peoples are lost no
More, for they are no more, and we
Wonder what has been found.

WORLD CUP – QATAR 2022

A Festival of Football, it was called,
A celebratory Feast, a Football-Fest,
Yet for all there was to savour, so little
To digest. For once more, once more,
Something is rotten at the core – when
The End, the prize, the outcome is so
Magnified, decked in such confected,
Transcendent Fame and Glory, that to
This End any Means, however foul,
Will do. It seems to matter not, how
Counterfeit the Glory, how hollow the
Fame – so am I left with scraps I cannot
Eat: It pays, it pays, it pays, to cheat.

The penalty 'box' is a box of tricks, for
Jostling and shoving at corner kicks—
And fabricating penalty-kicks – attackers
Falling, without being tripped; desperate
Defenders, to deny a goal, felling attackers
On purpose, knowing how often penalty
Kicks are saved, or missed: How often
It pays, it pays, to cheat.

Never mind the ball, go for his feet;
Yellow cards which should be red, so
Often does it pay, to cheat.
Persistent displays of histrionics, feigning
Pain, injured innocence, and hostile
Appeals to the Referee when decisions
Do not go their way – all disgrace the
Name of this Game, match after match.
And further to disgrace – disgust—
Disgust in relentless Machismo spitting,
Inseparable from the modern professional
Game, it seems. Spitting! Hallmark of
Heroic grit: See how football warriors
Spit, in the face of impossible odds.

My indigestion was somewhat relieved
As the Football-Fest ended, for the Final
Served up a fine display of high-quality
Football, relatively free of corruption, as
Always should be.

For sport must be sporting or it is
Nought – a good-natured contest of
Talent and skill – a contest, not a brawl.
It is a way of proving ourselves,
Reminding ourselves of the best we
Can be, as Humanity.

'Professional Sport' would seem a
Contradiction, for sport must be
Recreation, entertainment, and joy.
Its essence must be purely in the
Playing: Winning or losing, purely
In the playing too – afterwards of
No consequence at all.

TRESPASS

If I am not scooping algae from
My pond, I am pruning my shrubs,
Clipping my hedges, strimming
Verges or spraying weeds muscling
Through my concrete paths.
If I'm not tackling molehills on my
Borders, I'm culling slugs, caterpillars,
Snails; treating for greenfly and moss,
While ivy swarms over my walls, ants
Invade my patio – and spiders, large
Spiders, colonise my garden shed.
Mice in the attic, where floorboards
Are treated for woodworm; everywhere
Flies, except on the flypaper.

According to the Deeds, by ancient,
Solemn Statute, this miniscule plot of
England belongs, exclusively, to me—
But the Human Writ appears not to
Run beyond our human kind – a crass
Effrontery, validity unknown to the
Lawless laws of the living world.

Moot Points, ownership, inheritance
Of land – Moot Points then, I suppose.

With every scoop of algae, clipping of
Shrubs, spraying of weeds, setting of
Traps, I cannot but think that perhaps
I have a Case to Answer: I seem not
Welcome here.

Perhaps, in truth, I am the intruder
Here; if not the vermin, perhaps I
Am the Usurper, the Trespasser here.

INTEGRITY

It is to their constituency supporters
That Members of Parliament owe
Their status and the privileges thereof,
From which we might expect the
Judgements of their supporters, their
Electors, to be valued by MP's, and
Held in great respect.

It ain't necessarily so.

For once elected, they seem to join
Another, detached and superior 'party',
The 'Parliamentary Party', with its
Own implicit powers: It was these
They deployed, quite recently, in this
Democratic parliament of ours.

In a fine display of integrity, they
Would, from their own parliamentary
Ranks, suggest a successor to the
Leader they'd recently deposed.

A series of internal votes soon cut
Down the candidate numbers to two,
A He (Sunak) and a She (Truss), with
Their votes showing, clearly, preference
For the He.
In a fine display of impartiality, the
Choice between the two would be
Put to the Conservative Party at large.

But it weren't necessarily so.

For though MP's were favouring He,
The party at large voted, clearly, in
Favour of She.

Frustratedly, the Parliamentary Party,
Democrats all, looked on while as
Prime Minister She was installed—
At which the Parliamentary Party's
Bluff had been called.

For without the backing of her MP's,
She cannot effectively govern, see?
From the outset, they resisted, they
Sulked and despised.

Forty-nine days it took them, to bring
Her down – that lady elected to office
By voters akin to those who had made
Them into MP's.

Forty-nine days, to have their own ways,
And install the He of their choice – in
Defiance of their Party at large:
As Honourable Members, they refer to
Themselves.

But it ain't necessarily so.

BELL

Over the ether, out of the air,
A distant bell resounds, wordless
But clarion-clear, in significance
As much as in primitive tone:
It does not direct us, but calls
To us, appeals, in elementary form;
Bell-sound, shorn of irrelevance,
Encoded simplicity, language profound,
In meaning that we know so well,
So much more than we can tell.

Roosting in our towers and steeples
It calls, it chimes, heartbeat of a town,
Its peoples, forever measuring time,
Old years out, new ones in, neutral,
Impartial, that we may interpret how
We will, in the rafters of our minds.
Into our minds it delves, heart-reminder
 Of ourselves: Seems we have invented
Bells to interrogate ourselves, so to
Contemplate heavens and even hells.

INDECISION

Which is to be preferred, an 'eloquent
Silence' or a 'damning with faint praise'?
On balance, I'd choose the silence, I
Think, for here is scope to furnish
Something favourable to my mind;
In that silence I may quietly find some
Comfort.
A prime example, hardly 'damning',
But of the 'faint praise' variety, popped
Up when my daughter, having met,
For the first time, a friend of mine,
Declared that 'She seems quite nice'.
Had an unkind twist of fate not rendered
This their only meeting, I'm sure further
Wording would have thawed, but their
Only meeting it proved to be.
As neutral and flat enough was 'nice',
To describe my friend, just so 'quite'
Hardly gave it life or substance; still
Less did that cautious offering 'seems',
To which I so often fall prey myself.

Of course it was forgivable, in the
Circumstances; first impressions can
Be lasting ones if they are the only ones.
Never would I impute to my daughter
Any but the kindest of motives – and
Of course it would feel improper simply
To offer her Dad an 'eloquent silence',
Apt to be misconstrued.

I recall that moment simply to ponder
Many such, in life, when at short notice
We must offer some words, or maintain
A tactful silence: Hazards lie ahead of
Either option.
Upon reflection, come to think of it, as
Readily as comfort, suspicion often floats
Upon a silence – while words of faint
Praise, if falling short, do make some
Attempt to mollify.
Context may be everything, but being an
Indecisive sort of man, even less sure am
I now, to which I incline, than when I began.

Upon further reflection, I felt, before
The above was published I had better
Seek, secure, Daughterly Imprimatur:

Immediate, unequivocal, came her reply,
Making quite a case for eloquent silence:
"I didn't like her".

ORIENTATION

There's a right-way-up for maps and
Globes, for night-time skies and
Astronomical charts, to hold at bay
This insecurity of ours – conventions
Of our making and salvation, for
No 'up' is there, no 'down', no North
Nor South, East nor West, anywhere
In space out there.

We, the pivot of our compass, radiate
Bearings as if to find and locate our
Very selves in the vast indifference
Where reason, cause, much speculated,
Never may be found.

Why take it upon ourselves? Must we,
Like Atlas, bear it upon our shoulders?
We, here, around our Earthly home,
May sail our seas with relative ease,
Thanks to Mercator's projections in
Straight and parallel lines.

But he was aware, and so are we,
That Earth was projected imperfectly,
Distortedly; no more may surfaces of
Spheres be flattened than circles may
Be squared; still less may Geometry
Delineate the likes of you and me.

Long, as we must, for harbour lights,
There is no navigable chart for this
Lost human mind; in this are we
Essentially blind. Voyage as we may
In minds through space, its emptiness
Must be the right way up, its shores
Washed by salty seas, while in the
Minds of the likes of you and me,
The music of the spheres rings
Familiar harmonies, returning to
The Earth's 'Home Quay', that we
May sail familiar seas, and trust
Our providential deities.

TADPOLE

Somewhat bumbling and green by
Name: Tadpole, uncertain, barely
Begun, from the earliest miniscule
Stretch and twitch, as if to relieve
Some insistent itch; it doesn't know
It but it clearly has a mission – a
Somewhat clumsy body with tail,
All you really need – mere spasm
Of life, promising, clearly has a
Mission, busy in a blind kind of
Hope, potential and poignancy
Too: So, so few will metamorphose,
And those which do, before they
Perish, will but breed and spawn,
That several thousand tadpoles
More, blindly may be born.

In a way, since, all tadpoles I see
Are those first tadpoles I saw:

Those first tadpoles as a young
Boy I saw, seething in that shady
Pond, down that slope where my
Left shoe, loosened by a tree-root,
Tumbled down and plopped —
Scattering tadpoles and out of
Sight forever – perchance to mark,
Record for me, that seminal tadpole
Moment.
Tadpole; tadperson, personpole; the word evokes.

Many a mile since, have I limped
With that foot unshod, enraptured
By that tadpole god – as good a
Guide, I'd say, as any other gods,
Win or lose against the odds and
Tumbling shoes – metamorphosed
As Tadpole, a somewhat clumsy
Body, with diminishing tail, all
I really need, clearly on a mission,
Succeed or fail.

FORGIVENESS

Just how is a cuckoo supposed to know
How to build a nest? It is but the product
Of a lineage knowing nothing, and caring
Nothing, of building nests – genetically
Disposed to let sillier birds build nests—
Gullible little birds, like pipits, dunnocks
And warblers, who make the handiest
Of nests – sneak an egg into several of
Them, and let each cuckoo hatchling
Do the rest.
Of course, 'sillier', 'gullible', 'sneak', in
This context, will not do.

Every bit as blamelessly then, in a simple,
Blameless amorality, will each fat cuckoo
Hatchling shove any egg of pipit, dunnock
Or warbler over the rim of the nest, so
That it alone may be raised by a hapless
Foster-mother so deceived, and bereaved.

What then, of those tiny, fragile eggs
Of pipit, dunnock, warbler, sent
Plummeting down to the fertile soil?

If to forgive is to excuse, and understand,
With a generosity of heart, then in
This Matriarchy of ours, our Mother
Earth, we have no finer exemplar.

I have heard it rumoured, persuasively
Rumoured so, around the woodlands
And the meadows, that unbeknown to
Man or beast, every single promise of
A fledgling pipit, dunnock, warbler,
Far from being abandoned, is succoured,
Honoured, rooted and raised, in perpetuity,
As a Flower of Salvation and Forgiveness.

And by their very names, two of them
Bear witness to this wonderful Truth—

Of blamelessness, forgiveness,
Reassuring hints in our 'Lords
And Ladies', politely known as
Cuckoo Pints – with the innocence
Of Eden there laid bare;
Just as in the garment of our
'Lady's Smock' we admire as
Our Cuckoo Flower, what simple
Modesties are there.

Cuckoo Pint, Cuckoo Flower,
Blamelessness, forgiveness, by
A certain natural justice are
We bound; within apparent
Wantonness, so often simple
Sense and virtue found.

'MOLES'

The most amazing thing, about this
Utterly preposterous and least believable
Of phantoms, is that they've actually
Given it a Latin name, Talpa Europaea—
Believe it or not – and even dreamed
Up a simple rustic name, 'Mole', for
Simple folk like you and me.

Patronising, I know, but we have to be
Tolerant with People of Faith, and if
Ever there was an act of Faith, it must
Be this : In the countryside all around
Us, there are four-legged, air-breathing
Mammals, about the size of fat sausages,
With front paws like shovels, that spend
Their lives tunnelling underground in
Pursuit of their favourite delicacy, raw
Earthworms, occasionally relishing insect
Grubs as well.

As a life-long introvert myself, keeping
Well out of the limelight, I do feel a
Certain kinship, you know, with those
'Moles', but I wouldn't take it quite
That far.
It is not given to the likes of you and me
Actually to witness and verify in the
Flesh an incarnation of one such immortal
Carnivorous sausage, but as with other

Freakish cults, there will be the odd
Self-acclaimed eye-witness. I've seen
Their speculative sketches of their
Apparitions, even comically touched-up
'Photos' of what they have in their
Benighted minds.

I suppose if not to pity them, the kindest
Thing is to humour them. What are
They hiding from, those so-called 'Moles'?
Haven't they heard, the War is over?
Are they fugitives from the Law?
What murky secrets have been found,
By Mole Intelligence Five, to keep those
Guilty phantoms sculking underground?
Being nocturnal is one thing; permanently
Tunnelling is quite another. Oh, and
I've read that they are excellent swimmers.
Well, they would be, and no doubt they
Fly pretty well too.
And I've heard it said, by true Believers,
That those little clumps of soil, dotting
Our meadows, are thrown up by these
'Moles', when more likely they are the
Involuntary voidings of hapless earthworms,
Terrified out of their wits – hardly
Surprising, come to think of it, if you are
Constantly on the run from savage,
Carnivorous, phantom sausages.

RASPBERRY

At the risk of an awkward smile or
Laugh, indelicate would it be, by half,
To approach my topic by the nearest
Route, rather than reach for a substitute.
So it is to Old Cockneys I turn, for
Their echoing rhymes, their humorous
Hearts, and sweeten my subject – our
Raspberry Tarts.
Upon this my pencil never would dwell
If I wrote for a hundred years – but
That after a gap of fifty or so, I was
Invited to a local Christmas Panto.
Based on various nursery tales, the
Pantomime so helps to lift the curtain
On who we British are – our traditional
Letting-Go, our licence to laugh at
Ourselves, caricature, lampoon, with
Men playing Dames and girls playing
Princes, dressed-up truths so worth
Preserving; the exuberance of the
Amateur, the community spirit, and
All those stock characters too –
You know, like that friendly old
Pantomime cow, played by two
Intrepid Troupers, front-end standing,
Back-end bending down; mute and
Out of sight they always are, dangling
That bloated, prize-winning udder.

That udder itself, in my earlier days,
Was enough for a maidenly blush—
Even to speak its name, let alone its
Function: To quip that 'one good churn
Deserves an udder' – enough to flutter
The calmest of hearts.
Accustomed we were to mild innuendo
And the saucy 'double-entendre', but
How ill-prepared was I, fifty years on,
At the local Christmas Panto.

Forget the udder-function of the cow;
She serves some modern, blunter
Purpose now: Every time she's on the
Stage, the cow is there to split the air,
Pollute the air, with ostentatious
Venting of wind – Festive Bovine
Raspberry Tarts – way beyond the
Scope of the back-end Trouper
Bending down – these were heartily
Rendered and amplified, to reverberate
Though the House loudspeakers, over,
Over and over again,
("lest you should think she never could
Recapture the first fine careless rapture")

Lest we should miss the point, whatever
It was, the theatrical value in the Producer's
Mind, to all those young children there,
Of Festive, Bovine, Raspberry Tarts.

Was he striking some blow for freedom?
Blazing some trendy new trail?
Whatever his purpose, I found myself in
Deep despair, nonplussed and disappointed there.

What can I do now, remembering that
Cow and her Raspberry Tarts, but
Turn to Old Cockneys again and sigh,
At the spoiling of such a fine evening
By this sort of Pony and Trap?

EPH

How the sixteenth and the eighth
Letters in our alphabet came to
Represent the sixth, I have not the
Phaintest idea — thank goodness
This aphphectation hasn't spread
Much phurther through our
Language: Phor a start, it would
Phoul up the phonetic alphabet;
How could the letter 'eph' be
Phoxtrot? And phurthermore, iph
Every 'eph' sound had to conphorm
To this ophphicial phormat, the phuture
Would look phorbidding indeed—
The phinal nails in the cophphins
Carrying ophph phree speech and
Inphormality.
I hope you would join phorces with
Me, to phight against any phurther
Aphphronts to our Native Tongue
By phaceless Rephormers.
"Phreedom Phrom Artiphicial 'Ephs', I cry—
"Rally round the Phlag!"

JEAN

She is not Katriona, nor Fiona, not Esmée
Nor Esmeralda, Felicity nor Philomena;
She has no need to be, for she is Jean.
She is no Debutante, nor Dame, no
Princess, Countess, nor Lady-in-Waiting
To the Queen; she was never born to be,
For she is Jean.
She is no Harridan nor Super-model, no
Heroine nor Star, no Celebrity nor Household
Name; oh, mercifully not she; she is Jean.
Never to imply, of course, that along with
Title, Name or Spurious Fame, character
And virtue simply may not coincide –
But always to remind ourselves that
Respectability and worth lie independently
Of these – never to be added or awarded,
Like medals, but intrinsic within such
As my good friend, Jean.

When you come across natural goodness
And unselfishness, you know it: I came
Across it in Jean, and very soon, I knew it.

So far is she beyond any lyrical language
Of mine, that for a woman of good sense,
Benign temperament, and homespun
Wisdom, no contrivances, but plain words
Are due.
Born into a farming family, tending
And nurturing have been her life; early
And late lending a hand, earning a simple
Living from our land – as close as can be
To basic necessity, and fundamentals, a
Sense of living grounded and understood,
As to leave no space at all for airs and
Graces, fecklessness or foibles.

Nothing of the sort, but service to her
Family and her many friends; a love of
Life, a love of people, always at hand
To help, contribute and care – in Jean
A constancy, a quiet cornucopia of goodwill.

ANNA

Clearly, I am not quite beyond redemption,
For Anna, a Witness of whom Jehovah
Should be proud, still calls, from time to
Time. Always, she has a companion, for
Witness and security I imagine, who stands
A little way behind, sometimes adding a
A supporting word or two.
Always, she asks after my well-being, with
A sincerity impossible to doubt. She hands
Me the latest copy of 'Watchtower', often
Drawing my attention to an uplifting
Passage in her Bible.
She knows, from times past, that I am a
Natural atheist, unlikely to be converted,
But her mission for Jehovah is true, and
Admirable. Far from being a reason to
Pass me by, and try another door, my
Atheism seems as a challenge, again to
Try, that I may yet be turned, to see the
Light.

Each visit is an exquisite, and mutually
Respectful ten minutes or so, spiced by
Her courteous foreign tones (Czech),
Her patient commitment and oddly,
That my conversion to the Faith is as
Unlikely as her rejection of it.
Perhaps her fulfilment is contained
Enough in her dedication to her task
In the Faith.

Exquisite, I say, in the sheer civility, so
Often lacking in public discourse: Two
Views, totally opposed, aired with good
Grace, and not a trace of rancour—
Courtesy and respect on both sides,
Agreeing to disagree.
For arguments to be turned into quarrels,
There should never be need.
If such rapport were the norm, in all
Encounters of opposing views this world
Over – Jehovah's work and Anna's
Mission would surely be done – His
Millennial Kingdom Come.

I'm sure there are moral issues from
Which nobody would dissent, but
They are few and so, on most, views
Must be aired and shared – our Coming-
Of-Age as civilised beings by these
Grown-up means declared.
Peace on Earth: Hope Springs Eternal.
Let it not hurt our pride, that someone
Should take the opposing side.

Let the Householders of this world
Greet the Annas at their door, with
All good grace, and in their minds
Let there be space, to accommodate,
In a World of Peace, all viewpoints
Of the Human Race.

LIFELINES

It must have been our long-drawn-out,
Unprecedented dawning, that enforced
Upon us this long-drawn-out, unprecedented
Spawning – of this litter, unimagined
For the want of any imagination to
Conceive it: As much as to say, these
Fairies, these imps and gnomes, these
Goblins, leprechauns and these elves,
Are but aspects of ourselves.
Our tying-up of loose ends, I suppose
This all is: However tempting it may be,
To think that we awoke to these fairies
Waiting for us here in Fairyland, amazed
To find such orphaned mortals in their
Midst – ours is the parentage of course;
This litter, these offspring but to give
Some shape and form, to allay some
Fears, fill voids, locate and understand
Ourselves, as with families and friends,
A kind of tidying and tying up loose ends.

A childhood raised on fairy-tales, it
Follows, is a sustenance by nature, a
Nourishing of thoughts, imaginations,
Which otherwise might be starved,
Somewhat loose, and adrift.

My own hapless mother, effectively orphaned
And fostered – for all her dutiful caring
Of us – had thus, in infancy, been cast adrift.
Beyond the standard nursery-rhymes,
We encountered little: Only in later years
Did we come across the tales of the
Brothers Grimm, Lewis Carroll, Kenneth
Grahame, A A Milne – all, in our home,
 Summarily eschewed as 'Tripe'.

Lifelines, I'm sure that's what they are,
These Fairy-Figures, no less than lifelines,
Uncanny images of ourselves, helping
Explain the inexplicable, helping us to
Tell our Tale, one way to immortality
And an offering to posterity.

MINSTREL

At the time of my writing, and
Unbeknown to me, along Lea Bailey
Lane there was a dimming of a
Light, the ebbing of a life and a
Voice which had brought so much
Fun and joy, over his long and
Generous life, not only to Foresters
All, between Two Rivers, but out
And about, far and wide: It was
Mentioned, so sadly, to me—
Had I heard? Old Dick Brice had died.

A late arrival in this area, I had never
Met this man, but palpable his
Reputation hereabouts, as a Forester,
Root and branch.

However far and wide they stray,
It falls to the likes of Old Dick Brice,
Our minstrels, our bards, to know
Of us, tell of us in their songs, spice
And sauce our lives with humour,
Lift our spirits, help us cope and
Hope – as worthy a purpose as
Ever can be.

Any sense of mourning, I dare say,
In the minds of his Forest Brethren,
Will be flavoured with smiles and
Thankfulness, for the comradely
Light he shone – and echoes of his
Words and tunes will surely linger
On, now that Old Dick Brice is gone.

TROUBLES

As I write, remembrances are in the air.
Fortuitous of course, but yet how ominous,
That the Agreement was signed, twenty-five
Years ago on Good Friday, and not on
Easter Sunday: Crucifixion, not Resurrection,
Was the anniversary of the ending of the
'Troubles'. It's that word, 'Troubles'
Which so transfixes me. In Northern Ireland,
Twenty-something years before that signing,
Simmering tensions between Nationalist
And Unionist factions had boiled over:
Hatred between them seemed to know no
Bounds, though split between worshippers
Of the same Christian God of Love.

In its merciless torturing, maiming, bombing
Indiscriminately in public places, and summary
Executions, it terrorised a generation of
People, and showed utter contempt for their
Laws; it was a glimpse of mankind at his
Infernal worst.

Who on Earth would christen such a
Passage in our history as 'The Troubles'?
Difficulties, inconveniences, obstacles,
Floods, disputes, strikes maybe – but
Not a bloody campaign of hatred, in
Which over three thousand souls died.

If such can be described as 'Troubles',
Then words have lost their meanings,
And writers write in vain.

But this, I suspect, is no description, no
Soothing euphemism: I suspect this is
A menace, a chilling warning, wrapped
As a harmless understatement:
Think of those events as mere 'Troubles',
And try to imagine what we're capable of
If you get in our way again.

MASQUERADE

If they are so confident, so proud
And self-possessed, those 'gurus'
On the Opinion Pages, to stare us
Unblinkingly in the face, week after
Week, they surely have a treasure-
House of words to say, infinite wit
And wisdom to help us mortals on
Our way.
I marvel at their sense of themselves:
No head-and-shoulders images for
They, but full-length, casually posed,
Like mannequins preened, or casually
Seated, as homely Oracles to put us
At our ease. Pretty substantial egos
To begin with, I should say, ever to
Offer themselves, puff themselves,
In such a brazen way – wonderful
Self-belief; divinities but Earthbound,
From whose Notebooks and Diaries
We may expect a world of calm philosophy;
Libraries of wisdom from whose lips.

But wait – oh dear – again, once
Again, I fear; I find, in this mean
Hyperbole, that taste, yes that old
Familiar vinegary taste, known to
Aesop's hungry fox and not unknown
To introverts like me:

Could it be that , in scoffing at such
Exposure, too eagerly we see talents
As vanities, confidence as arrogance,
All accomplishments as disorders?

Could it not be just human nature's
Way – our deficiencies and envies
Thus are overlaid, superficially unseen
Behind this, our critical masquerade?

COURTESY

Flat, and lacking, was her voice,
As if as bored was she, as were we.
At no point did she address her
Lecture directly to us. Showing us
For one hour, slides of modernist
Paintings, she read from a script
At the lectern, microphone in her
Left hand. Any moment you took
Your eyes off the slides, you would
Find her right hand twirling the
Air, as if to seek assistance there, as if
To help unravel the mystery and
Artistry of those paintings, that
We should be enlightened.
Nor did it inspire much confidence
That several slides were simply
Passages those artists had written,
Which she obligingly read out for
Us. Essentially borrowed, therefore,
Was her narrative, distinctly lacking
In freshness and coherence.

Whatever her fees were, I felt at
The time, she had over-charged.

Possibly, she was insensitive to this,
And may well have missed the bare
Politeness in the applause when she
Had finished – an uneasy stillness
In the hall – into which stepped our
Chairman, as relieved as anybody,
I dare say, whose task was to be as
Gracious as any British chap should
Be.
Sincerely, I feel sure, did he thank
The lady for her excellent enlightening
Talk: For courtesy is unblemished
Or it is nought; knowing nothing of
Disapproval, it is born of good manners
And consideration, to put all people
At their ease – such the overriding
Sentiment from our Chairman,
Which saved our day.

Allowing in this way, that the lady
Had done her very best, for which
Nothing but praise will do, and
Allowing us to ask ourselves how
Often it is our very best that we all
Routinely do.

No question at all that our Chairman's
Instincts were right, that dull and
Barren afternoon thereby saved, and
Bathed in a brighter light.

CORONATION, CHARLES III

Just how all our preceding British
Monarchs made their coronation vows,
I do not know.
Nor is there any sense in knowing:
History is worth studying, and
Knowing, but so much of Crown
And Nationhood is of sentiment—
Conceptual, immaterial, an array
Of tradition and loyalty, that details
Of procedures matter so much less
Than what they represent.

As foreshadowed in Nineteen
Fifty-three, this coronation was
Televised and scrutinised by sound
And sight, for the world to watch
And for posterity, repeatedly, to see.

At every point, from every height
And angle, microphones and cameras
Guided us through but, I'm bound
To say, further and deeper than
They needed to, further than was
Wise, for the essence of a coronation
Lies well beyond the people's eyes.

The accoutrements of office, so
Charged with symbolism, were
Better spoken of than enacted in
That over-literal, unconvincing way;
The placing of crowns upon royal
Heads is risk enough to solemnity
And dignity.

All the pomp and pageantry, all
The soaring, proud and reverential
Music; all was purposed, and a
Prelude to, one brief and solemn
Moment, that transcendent moment
Of the Monarch's personal oath of
Lifelong service to the people.
Through those insatiable cameras,
We were right there, at the Monarch's
Side to witness – not a personal,
Heartfelt pledge but, from cue-cards
Held out before him, someone else's
Words prescribed.
Bathos.
This great day in our Nation's story,
Remembered now for hollowness
At its core, the oath of office, memorably
If not mortally undermined, by
Contrivance of this faint-hearted kind.

To deliver personally, authentically,
The oath of office, should be well
Within the courage and compass of
Any Monarch at coronation.
Who knows whether all preceding
Monarchs learned their lines and
Personally delivered them?
I hope they did, but I'd rather not
Know, than be aware of this latest,
Modern travesty.

TOUCHSTONES

A touchstone, it would appear to be, for
Such as weekly write the columns, or surf
The airwaves, a touchstone of indelicacy,
It would appear to be – freed from decency
And gentle euphemism – a pretentious
Modern Social Order, indelicacy its badge,
Impropriety its membership card.
Even more than the words 'poo' and 'wee'
I saw on my GP's notice board – for the
Barely literate peasantry – theirs is the
Lexicon of liberation, never to be tied by
Sweet or coy convention: Far be it from
Them to 'spend a penny'; they prefer to go
For a pee, or even to rhyme it with 'this'—
As with a going-to-the-toilet Number Two,
Preferring to allude to exactly what they're
About to do.
'Bum' is a name too tame, for a bottom; arse,
Or the transatlantic 'ass' is tougher by far—
And see how those people never refer to the
Breaking of wind, but always, always, sound
It as raspberry tart.
Let no notion of tenderness or nursing
Restrain this avant-garde: Never 'teat' nor
Its brief derivative will do; in this free-born
Social Order a breast must be a 'boob'.
Irresistible too, our genitalia: In days gone
By, rather disowned as 'private parts'—
Touchstones aplenty for the freer spirits.

Notwithstanding the proper, respectable
Names for His and Hers, endless scope for
Indelicacy, from playful to embarrassing
And to gratuitously coarse.
And when it comes to our inborn call to
Mate, to procreate, all words fail, and fall well
Short, in the arid, de-personalising term of
'Having Sex' – even the gentle phrase of
'Making Love' falls well short, we know:
What then for the card-carrying members of
The Modern Social Order, who render such
Moments through the F-word, the S-word, or
Even the fatuous label 'bonk' – aversion to
Finer feelings maybe, emotional cowardice
Of some kind.
Their touchstones are travesties, not strengths,
I suspect, but certain weaknesses of mind.

NEWS

Depressing has been the morning
News this week: One country
Persecuting Christians, another
Tormenting Jews; relentless war
In Central Europe; knife attacks
On our city streets; hangings in the
Middle East; landmines, poisonings,
Nuclear missile tests; dissenters
Jailed; freedoms brutally suppressed;
Violent protests; race riots –- tension,
Turmoil, even in democracies.

A little later on, each weekday
Morning, has been a Natural History
Series – butterflies on Monday, then
Giraffes, dolphins, toads and kangaroos.
This Series was entitled "Wildlife".

POP

We brought it upon ourselves, you know,
Upon our too-self-conscious selves – this
Precious fear of Nakedness – as if we were
Incomplete, from our chins to our feet,
Without an extra skin or hide, to conceal
Ourselves here inside – apparel, dress,
Protective clothing.

Readily enough, to Mums and Dads, very
Close friends, and lovers, will we loosen
Off the extra hide, that they may attend
To what's inside. But like it or not, there's
Another lot, the medical lot, whose access,
Now and then, has to be implied. Here
Lies the difficulty: Without the Mum or
The Dad, the friend or the lover, you are
'Patient', to uncover.

"Strip off, undress for me", might seem
Rude, potentially misconstrued.

"Let me have a look in here", can only
Mean an unprofessional leer.
"Lie back on the bed" – oh, helpless dread.

Stark, or even partial, Nakedness is
Nemesis, our human undoing.
Thank goodness then, and all praises
Due, to our Sisterhood of Nurses,
Resourceful as they always are.
They have perceived our plight, and
Ingeniously put things right: Make it
Sound less like a command, more of
A friendly request, adding a spoonful
Of sugar to their words, by bringing
To bear (or bringing to bare) this
Ubiquitous, versatile, sweetener,
Adapting the emollient, jolly little
Verb, "to pop":
"Pop y'self on the bed a moment".
"Pop y'top off for me".
"Pop y'bottom on here".
"Pop this under there".
"Pop y'pants down and let me have a look".
Balloons of embarrassment, gently popped.

SHAKESPEARE

Such an implied compliment it is, to
William Shakespeare, that four centuries
After his death, we continue to read and
Watch his Plays.
How they develop, how they end, we
Full well know, but again and again we
Turn to them, for in so many of their
Acts and Scenes, we perceive ourselves.
Through his wisdom, his wizardry in
Words, his awareness of us all – we
Perceive ourselves.
Productions of Macbeth have I seen—
Maybe eight or nine times. The weakest,
And most frustrating, was at Stratford,
For without the Three Witches, but
Three young children instead – the
Dialogue modified to suit – the whole
Tension of the Play was deflated.
It was an affront to the reputation of
Shakespeare.

This is a more modern, and far less
Forgivable fashion than staging his Plays,
With all their Elizabethan idioms and
Allusions, in 21st century settings and
Dress – the justification, that his work
Is inherently timeless – being precisely
The reason modern settings are not
Needed.

I read recently of a new production
At Stratford, for which the 'Porter'
Scene is being re-written, to be more
Amusing for modern audiences—
A tiresome, vexing liberty – an affront
Which should be an indictable offence
Against some Eternal Copyright.

The Royal Shakespeare Company,
Being Royal, we might expect to be
Unswervingly Loyal, to the man in
Whose name and reputation they trade.

To stage a Play to the best dramatic
Effect, is a Producer's task, not to amend
It to promote and satisfy himself. How
Dare he? What conceit and arrogance
It must take, to superimpose yourself
On a Shakespeare Play, and sell it as
A fake. Leave this man's works and words
Alone; write works and wordings of
Your own.

In the particular case of Macbeth, by all
Means adjust it here and there, write in
Your own bits here and there—
But Do Not You Ever Dare,
Do Not You Ever, Ever Dare,
To promote it as 'Macbeth'.
Call it by some other name, however much
Or little you amend — as West Side Story
Is to Romeo and Juliet.

And Do Not You Ever Dare,
Do Not You Ever, Ever Dare,
To attribute your disfigured version
To William Shakespeare.

IMMUTABILITY

Organisms, that's what we are: Living
Is not what we do; it's what we are—
'Biological', the 'logical' being tried and
Tested in Nature's way.
Without discernible origin, our heritage
Has been millennially slow, incremental,
But being a matter of natural, incidental
Adaptation through the ages, has wrought
Only those changes which made for our
Survival – successful replication of our kind.
We are tried and tested in Nature's way,
From which process, evidently blind, as
Male and female are we assigned.
With due exceptions, came a General Rule:
Larger, louder, more aggressive He; more
Practical, intuitively wiser She.

Along came rationality, and cultures, to
Test and try us in a newer way, with new
Moralities and customs, to take to task
What evolution had to say.

A logic of new-found Reason, too often
Counter to what Nature had to say, breeds
So many dilemmas of today.
Organisms versus Reason.

With Nature being so senior and immutable,
When She and cultures find themselves
At odds, it is we who have to justify ourselves,
Our admiration of ourselves, our pretensions
To power, our destiny, and most telling
Of all, our Gods.

All of which is built on sand, and ultimately
Will not stand. No more will spurious notions
Alter facts, and now that interchangeability
Between the sexes is the keynote of the day,
It might be worth our listening to what
Nature has to say.

SECURITY

We have a tendency to hide, we introverts,
To be unnoticed, private and quiet,
Keeping our thoughts inside. At whatever
Cost, never must we draw attention to
Ourselves, nor expose ourselves, Heaven
Forbid, to public spectacle or ridicule;
Embarrassment our Personal Dread.

Shuffling forward, in a lengthy queue,
Towards the airport security point,
Jean and I witnessed those ahead
Being monitored, questioned, and
Occasionally searched – a process so
Sadly necessary, in this world of ours
Today.
Into the trays, on the rollers, we placed
Our portable extras, to be screened by
The X-rays. Then Jean, more seasoned
A traveller than I, confidently made her
Way through.

But as for the likes of me, with a passive
Manner, an air of secrecy about us, and
Expressionless faces, I guess we introverts
Arouse suspicion: We have obviously
Something to hide.
Having no hand-luggage – it was to be
A short flight – I had only my jacket in
The tray.

But they had seen my type before: Shifty,
Dodgy, a cocky show of innocence and empty-
Handedness.

Walk through the gate: Alarm, go back.
Your watch must go in the tray.
Walk through again: Alarm, go back.
Hand over your coins.
Walk through again: Alarm, go back.
Walk through again: Alarm, go back.
Might be my braces, I suggested.
Take off your braces.
But my trousers?
You'll have to hold them up.
Walk through again: No alarm, go back.
Walk through again, to be sure: No alarm.
Having surrendered my braces, I stood,
Holding up loose-fitting trousers, while
The man expertly ran hands around and
Down and under, all in front of a hundred
Eyes in that slowly shuffling queue.

Isolated, lost, stranded, speechless, red-
Faced; embarrassment personified.
Aged eighty-five, I needed my Mum.

Desperately, I looked around for Jean;
Surely some succour and comfort there.

But there she was, barely able to stand,
Weak-kneed and tears rolling at such a
Comically-entertaining sight, her whole
Being convulsed, helplessly shaking with
Laughter.

Never in her life had she laughed so much,
Declared Jean.

INFILTRATORS

It is so voluntarily, and with such
Effrontery, in their hundreds, even
Thousands, that they reward the
Traffickers and covertly cross La
Manche, to claim asylum here.
It is also bogus, and illegal.

Routinely, our BBC garlands them
As 'asylum-seekers', though they are
Nothing of the kind: You do not seek
What you have already found. If you
Do not find asylum, sanctuary, in France,
It is not asylum that you seek.

Instead, you assume an entitlement that
Is not yours, a liberty to enter a country
Of your choice, in spite of its laws, caring
Nothing for the people into whose land
You voluntarily sneak.

To pay big money to criminals,
Chancing your lives in the crossing,
Shows not how desperate those people
Are, but how foolish, how opportunistic
And grasping.

No doubt many have landed undetected
Here, and will never be found, but for
Those who are taken in hand, identified,
Recorded, an immediate return to France
Would seem compulsory, and just,
Notwithstanding the BBC.

But our good neighbours across the channel
Will not receive the sneakers back.
Next-door neighbours, with such short
Memories, and so little conscience.

JERSEY

One, in particular, lingers, from all
Impressions of my first visit to Jersey,
That of several 'honesty-boxes' around
The island which, said our tour-guide
Are, without exception, respected and
Honoured. It is a matter of honour,
After all, appealing to the best within
Us, cultivated qualities of honesty and
Trust – a sense of decency and fairness.

The principle is simple, and an open
Invitation to a passer-by. Clearly
Marked is the price of each item for
Sale: Just leave your cash, and take
The item.

In practice, however, for the unscrupulous,
Temptation is laid bare. No one is around
To witness, if you simply take the item
And slide away.

As to personality, charisma, only in company
Can this be proved, but only on your
Own, as here, can character, moral strength,
Be truly tested; you are sole witness to
Yourself.
Fail this test, and bear it in your mind;
Pass this test, and walk tall.
No one will praise you, for no one will
Know, but you.
Only the seller will know if somebody
Failed the honesty-test.

Here in England, I have heard of such
Boxes similarly honoured, but also of
Several being abused, and so abandoned.

It is wonderful to be trusted; disappointing
To say the least, to see that trust abused.

A comparable impression, in Jersey, was
Of road junctions where two tributary
Roads fed into one at a roundabout:

The road sign said, 'Filter in turn'.
Simple, elegant, courteous way of
Avoiding frustration, fostering a
Feeling of community.

Maybe, to take a dim view of things,
In a small island community, there
Are fewer places to hide – or maybe,
To be called a 'community' has a
Natural limit in numbers: A city is
Not a community; there are various
'Communities' within it.
A population limit, there appears to
Be, beyond which trust fragments.

Explicit in 'community' is unity;
Implicit are neighbourliness, affinity.

No need has an honesty-box for keys
Or locks.
So may we build communities, without
The need for locks or keys, but bound
By Trust and Honesties.

CUDDLE

Our first experience, outside of the
Womb, is a barely conscious encircling
Of arms, a cuddling to the bosom, in
Arms – an imprint on our infant mind;
An imprint never lost, the likes of
Which we'll search this world to find.

Engendered so by such deep comfort,
Cuddling in mankind abides, insistently
In the mind, or why seek what's not
Lost, to find? By this, we might say,
Are we defined: Enfolding arms of a
Fond embrace, a spectral presence in
The human race.

In a sense – I'd go so far – our motherly
Embrace, inescapably, is what we are;
Fathomless inheritance, our motherly
Embrace, universal lingua franca for
A wandering human race.

How eager were we, to leave, wandering
Free at Nature's call; apparently free in
Individuality, our own private, personal
Space – all too soon to feel, in body and
Mind, the want of those encircling arms,
Something akin to the old embrace.

And so we search this world, as if to
Exercise a choice, but this be far less
Choice than giving in to that foreshadowed
In those encircling arms, old Nature's
Mothering voice.

Let us recognise ourselves, that we may
Sense our counterpart, meet our match,
Search and be found, reach out, be reached,
Tenderly touch, clasp, cleave. To this
Purpose only, did we leave.

We shall not wander far, if we are true
To what we are.

GOODNESS

All I had done, at the end of the Arts
Society lecture, was respond to an appeal
By a lady on behalf of her disabled mother,
For a lift to where they could catch their
Bus. It was not far, but the afternoon was
Hot, and the traffic busy.
It was just after I had dropped them off,
And headed for home, that this feeling
Flowed – brief, and satisfying – pleased
With myself – by their genuine gratitude
Briefly ennobled: Surprisingly odd feeling,
Having been kind – almost improper to
Feel pleased with myself, as if there is some
Unworthy, selfish motive in being kind.

Not to show what a wonderful fellow I've
Turned out to be, do I report this, but such
Kindred feelings to share, and ponder.
Do I offer help, ultimately, to please myself?
Funny thing that; funny thing this: Let's
Hope it's a blameless feeling simply because
In human terms, it seems 'right'.

This notion of kindness prompted a
Recall from several years ago, when a
Neighbour, having a small oak sideboard
Surplus to his needs, offered it, free, to
Me. Unwisely, on delivery, I offered
Some payment:
"Oh no" said he, "that would spoil the
Whole thing".

Of course he was right. Money would
Have sullied, degraded, commercialised,
The decency of the act.

Virtue surely is its own reward.
Then how to detach the reward as a
Motive, from the virtue?
That is the question.

STATUS

Hierarchy is what we have, as inevitable
As society itself – for better or for worse,
Blessing or curse, this is our inheritance.
One might wish our world as otherwise,
But thiswise it must be, with leaders and
Decision-makers, order-givers and order-
Takers – or there is no Order.
Many and varied are the strata, across
Professions and trades, but discernible
Still, even today, is a simple, ancient
Dichotomy, which lingers, stubbornly,
From times of aristocracy and peasantry:
Visible still, are remnants of a Ruling Class.
And being so, promotion can be less of
A gradual ramp, a hypotenuse, and more
Of a step-change, along and up, then along
At a status somewhat higher, a clear step-
Up, as it were, among the Rulers from
The Ruled – nowhere better illustrated
These days, than in the Armed Forces of
The Crown, where from the Non-Commissioned
You can be 'Commissioned'.

I write from my own experience – what
Better? I doubt it is known as such these
Days, but I joined the Royal Navy on the
'Lower Deck', naturally enough being, like
Most people, raised with limited expectations.
Eight years on, by dint of passing interviews
And written examinations, none at the first
Attempt, just about getting through courses,
And with a seasoning of good luck thrown
In, I was to be 'Commissioned'.

The document, 'By the Commissioners
For executing the Office of Lord High Admiral
Of the United Kingdom', is framed, and
Now hangs on my wall.
'By virtue of the Power and Authority
To us given by Her Majesty's Letters Patent
Under the Great Seal',

It appointed me as Sub-Lieutenant, and
Charged me

'To observe and execute the Queen's
Regulations and Admiralty Instructions
For the Government of Her Majesty's
Naval Service,'
And at the same time charges all those
Subordinate to me
'To behave themselves with all due Respect
And Obedience to you, their Superior Officer,'
Signed off in the 'Twelfth year of Her Majesty's
Reign'.
Subordinate to me! A young fellow raised
Unquestionably to be subordinate ('Keep your
Mouth shut and do as you're told') – with
Hardly a trace of authority, or even personality,
About me. And of course I remained subordinate,
For ever, to officer ranks above me.
I was to wear a finer uniform, with a grander
Cap-badge, to be waited upon at table, in
Separate quarters, with separate toilets, from
The Ratings. By Ratings was I to be addressed
As 'Sir', and furthermore to which I was so
Uncomfortably unsuited, by ratings was I to be—
Or rather the new uniform I wore was to be,
In passing, Saluted!
I never entirely got used to it; along with some
Personal pride, always a touch of embarrassment.
Against my nature, it was a matter of acting
The part.

To play my part in this tradition of loyalty and
Service, I was so proud, if so ill-prepared, finding
Myself among more 'chaps' than 'blokes', people
Wonderfully self-contained, by background and
Expectation so trained. By no means all, it
Was clear, but many were they 'to the manner
Born', with brisk authority in their voices—
Every utterance a certainty, even questions
More as demands than enquiries.
Orders, after all, must be Orders, not polite
Requests
How helpful it is, and was, where orders must
Be carried out promptly and efficiently, that
The chain of command usually works, that those
Obliged to follow orders, dutifully do so, to the
Gratification of those who issue them. Otherwise,
There is no Order.
Something in the nature, and status, of a Ruling
Class, I guess there must be, provided that the Ruling,
If not the Class, remains open to the likes of you and me.

IDIOM

What limp importers of American idiom
We are turning out to be – near to the
Point of surrendering, subordinating, our
Idiom to theirs.
Of our 'Special Relationship', one aspect
Would seem to be dependency – the
Cultural weakness of the borrower, the
Copier: Why bother to say 'Good Morning'
Or 'Hallo', when you can say 'Hi'?

Speaking of the 'fast lane' on our motorways,
When it is the traffic that is fast, not the lane,
We switch the epithet with some awareness
And sense – but of a motorway as 'Smart',
For goodness sake, wherefore can we speak?
As slavish and preposterous as 'smart meters'
In our kitchens. It is to prostitute the verb:
Neither motorway nor meter is stylishly
Dressed, nor conspicuously clever – crass
Transatlantic import.

Informality in slickness is the order of
The day; rather sad, what we gave away
When we lost forever our word 'gay',
From high-spirited to homosexual.
And even the word 'guy', as male, has
Whimpered away – androgynous now:
When Jean and I had studied the menu,
"Are you guys ready to order?" Useful

218

And functional words, melted down by
The Trendy.
'Guys', furthermore, do not come in
Groups now, but in 'bunches', rather
Like cut flowers. Witness what befalls
This language of ours.

Less and less do we 'have' a look; nowadays
We must 'take' a look in the true American
Way.
And we risk losing 'films' forever, giving way
To American 'movies'.
Why bother with a 'Cookery Book', when you
Can refer to a 'Cookbook' instead, and do all
Your frying in a 'Frypan'?

At least we've done well so far in resisting
'There you go' that would elbow aside our
'There you are'.

Before we routinely say 'sure', instead of
'Yes'; before 'Honey' becomes the endearment
Of habit and choice, it matters to me to
Hear again the English voice – to stem the
Tide, to man the barricades of our literacy—
To reinstate what we can of our wonderful
English language, and our precious native
Idiom.

EXCURSION

Back in my schooldays, in the nineteen-
Forties, if you had mentioned a 'coach',
It would have evoked a rather stately
Horse-drawn vehicle, used by wealthy
People, or similar ones in the cowboy
Films, pursued by bandits or wild Indians.

For the ones that took us on school trips,
To exotic places like Cheddar Gorge or
Stonehenge, we confidently knew as
'Sharrabangs'. This I now know was a
Corruption of 'char-à-banc', defined as
A long and light vehicle with transverse
Seats, looking forward; a motor-coach.
'Looking forward' encapsulates the
Experience, though I now look back,
Seventy years or so.
The memories came recently, when as a
Guest, I went on a coach-trip to Stratford-
Upon-Avon.

Although it did not occur to us to join
In lusty choruses of 'Ten Green Bottles
Hanging on the Wall, nor 'Ten Men Went
To Mow, Went to Mow a Meadow', there
Was a palpable communion for the day
About us, joined in looking forward,
Which brought back memories.
We just had to sit back and be taken,

Enjoy a sense of freedom for the day;
Anticipation too, free to gaze at passing
Fields and homesteads, share the occasional
Thought with companions – a welcome
Liberation from whichever routines
Governed our days.

Back then, having no memories, we knew
Only a 'looking forward': In our school
Uniforms, with our packed lunches, though
We were not volunteers, we were out of
The classroom, and though there was a
'Sir' and a 'Miss' teacher on each sharrabang,
There was a sweet smell of freedom, except
By chance, for the odd boy out, who had to
Sit by a girl – utterly mortified. I once did, and was.
Anticipation highlights all such journeys,
Vague and unformed hopes in those days;
Thoughtful expectations now. But even now,
As then, such an outing is a kind of therapy,
Some reassurance in a common, shared
Experience. Not the teachers in those days, calling for
Attention from the front, but now the likes
Of Gill Davis, who organised it all, informing
Us by microphone of departure and arrival
Times, the necessary 'comfort-breaks',
Organising the collection for the Driver, and
Drawing us all together on the homeward
Leg with a microphone game of Bingo.

These sharrabang days, then and now, are
But safe excursions, so their 'looking forward'
Know well of a homeward leg, whereof those
Children at school, and those same children
In retirement, may rest assured.
What the retired have learned, and the youngsters
Have yet to learn, is that excursions do not
Organise themselves: How we depend upon
Organisers and volunteers, and how lucky we
Are to live in a land of freedom and goodwill,
A land of Looking Forward.

IRONIES

Let us be upspoken enough to
Challenge the orthodoxies of our
Age, for notwithstanding Human
Nature, so many ways and policies
Assume an oddly inconsistent view,
And specialise in Ironies.

If your observations have not taught
You, what History books, what Papers
Have you ever read, which suggest to
You that people of very different cultures
Positively thrive cheek-by-jowl, in lasting,
Mutually-enriching harmony? Quite so.
Yet open immigration has been held up
As a touchstone of British virtue.
If this be so, virtue knows nought of
Sanity: 'Diversity' is our panacea.

On a par with this, comes Irony Number
Two, the Woman's Hour, Woman's Month,
Year, Everlasting Point of View, that
Masculinity is toxic, patriarchy an offence
Against Heaven, when it is no more
Than sound old Nature's way; no more
Should maleness be held in contempt
Than all the gentle blessings in femaleness.

Dear Ladies, this prevailing disposition
In the male, doth it not, within his nature
So inhere? You might as well despise the
Sun for shining, resent the lion his mane,
The stag his antlers, and deplore the
Plumage and dawn choruses of patriarchal
Songbirds.

Locally, as well as globally, Irony Number
Three relates to population density. The
Finite resources of this Earth should muffle
Any joy at any millionth birth. Yet here
And there we read of 'alarm' at some country's
Falling population, or the prospect thereof.

Birth Control now, is well within our
Comprehension and our means, but now we
Seem to delegate Control to pandemic
Diseases, to genocide, and wars, more willing
To tackle a symptom, than a cause.
So caught up in ourselves are we, that
The least tractable of all, is Irony Number
Four – that Human Life is sacrosanct, for
Which, I suppose, we may be forgiven,
And for which, I suppose, be thanked.

What Human lunacy it would be, to
Step aside, as it were, and let indifferent
Nature peg our numbers down – as with
All other forms of life – preserving in
Her harsh wisdom, the best that any kind
Can be. Cornered, as it were, inside of
Ourselves, we must cure the sick, relieve
The sufferers, and postpone death for
As long as we can.

Ironies all, to perplex us all, and make us
Wonder in what spirit – optimistic, humorous,
Despairing, wishful – did the classifiers of
Our Genus, Homo, following Linnaeus,
Designate our Species 'Sapiens'.

SHINING

Even today, the approach from Steam
Mills into Cinderford has a depressing
Drabness, a greyness and general dereliction,
To remind one of tough and rugged days
Gone by. For it is to coal, and steam
And manual labour, that Cinderford owes
Its character: Out of the collieries, the
Ironworks and railways grew a town one
Early writer described as 'a network of
Unlovely dwellings, mostly small, with
Shops of the co-operative class, where
Boots and bacon jostle each other, side-
By-side'.

A certain sadness there is, in looking back
Through local history, especially through
Early photographs, but always a kind of
Admiration too, for the stoical spirit of the
People, getting by and making do.

'In an ideal world' should never have to be
A phrase we ruefully use, but when we
Encounter bright exceptions to a background
Drabness, it is one we gratefully choose.
If an ideal world exists, it will not be found
In artefacts, or things, but in attitudes and
Minds. And so, from the general to the
Particular am I led by such thoughts, to this
Dentistry, in Cinderford.

As an outsider, known to nobody except, in
The course of their work, to Receptionist
And Dentist, I sit quietly in the waiting area,
Noticing patients, arriving and leaving.

The patients do not look prosperous. Dress
Is simply practical and functional. Bearing
Is that of takers, not givers, of orders; air
Of disadvantage, and resilience; some few
With disabilities. Mostly known to each other,
I dare say, at least by sight, they respect the
Ethos of the place, chatting only minimally.
But they all know Wendy, the Receptionist,
And Wendy knows them all, by friendly and
Familiar names.

In their brief checking-in and checking-out,
It is here, against the drab background of the
Town, in the clinical austerity of the waiting
Area, that the human spirit briefly shines.
Not one word of affectation is here, but well-
Wishing and good humour, at a common purpose,
In the charming, well-worn vernacular and
Dialect of this old industrial area. Something
Touching there is, in an unpretentious
 Ruggedness of spirit.

At her Reception Desk, Wendy is the very
Heart and pivot of the place, bright, efficient
And likeable – invaluable, I'd guess to the
Practising Dentists.

No less efficient and likeable, and no more
Native to the town than I, is my excellent
Dentist Isabel Bras: Engagingly unaffected
With her patients, she greets us all as friends.
A thoroughly competent practitioner, she
Explains and reassures, in her open, animated
Way, as if so natural, in the Portuguese,
To render people at their ease – as bright an
Exception to the drabness of the town, as
One would wish to meet.

From Steam Mills into Cinderford – for all
The 'unlovely dwellings' – this is much more
Than getting by, or making do, as through
Memories of hardship, poverty, and those
Merciless mines, the spirit of good people
Here, inborn, indomitably shines.